When the One You Love Wants to Leave

When the
One You
Love Wants
to Leave

Donald R. Harvey, Ph.D.

RAVEN'S RIDGE
B O O K S

BAKER BOOK HOUSE
Grand Rapids, Michigan 49516

Published by Baker Books
a division of Baker Book House Company
P.O. Box 6287, Grand Rapids, MI 49516-6287

Third printing, September 1994

Printed in the United States of America

Scripture quotations are from The New English Bible. © The Delegates
of the Oxford University Press and The Syndics of the Cambridge
University Press 1961, 1970. Reprinted by permission.

All names of persons whose stories are shared have been changed,
as have their situations, in order that privacy may be protected.

Library of Congress Cataloging-in-Publication Data

Harvey, Donald R. (Donald Reid).
    When the one you love wants to leave / Donald R. Harvey.
        p.   cm.
    ISBN 0-8010-4385-9
    1. Marriage—Religious aspects—Christianity. 2. Separation
(Law) 3. Divorce—Religious aspects—Christianity. I. Title.
BT706.H37   1989   89-8427
248. 8' 46—dc20

Contents

First Things First

In *When the One You Love Wants to Leave*, Dr. Donald Harvey shares his philosophy in confronting a broken marriage: "You must deal with the separation before you can deal with the marriage."

This book will help you to first uncover the reasons behind your spouse's departure. Then and only then will you be in a position to examine your marital relationship, honestly resolve the problems, and work together toward a genuine, lasting reconciliation.

When the One You Love Wants to Leave will help you to clearly evaluate your situation rather than let your emotions control your decisions. This way, you can face reality, work through feelings of guilt and fear, and take control of your life—with the ultimate objective of restoring your marriage.

Introduction

When the One You Love Wants to Leave is about marital separation. More importantly, it tells you what to do when you face separation—a book that was written in response to a very real need. Although separation is an event confronting many marriages, there is actually very little help available for couples painfully grappling with this crisis. Are there things that should be done? Are there other things that should be avoided? Are the rules for Christians different from those in the secular world? Is there a biblical model that deals with separation? These are but some of the questions answered by this book.

When the One You Love Wants to Leave is the product of two things. First, it is my desire to deal with marital crisis, even separation, in a redemptive manner. Certainly, most divorces are preceded by a separation, but all separations do not have to lead to a divorce. Even in times of extreme marital turmoil, there ought to be a plan of action that healthily pushes toward the goal of reconciliation. The second precipitant of this book was my own confusion regarding the "right" things to do in instances of separation. I found traditional marital therapy inadequate; in fact, it often hindered real progress. But what, if anything, would be better?

Over the past years I have acquired a mature appreciation for states of confusion. I say "mature" appreciation because who in their right mind would want to be confused? I can't say it feels good. But aside from its emotional discomfort, I can look back and see positive results because I have found confusion to be "growth ground." When I'm confused, I'm forced to learn, forced to resolve, forced to derive some order out of my chaos. Deriving order out of chaos is what occurred when I began grappling with the issue of dealing redemptively with marital separation.

Although each situation is unique, there are scriptural principles that bring commonality to all marital separations. Granted, there are no guarantees. As human beings, we are all damaged goods. Sometimes husbands make good decisions, sometimes they don't, and the same can be said for wives. But the fact remains that, regardless of outcome, there is a course of action that is best—best for the individual and best for the relationship. Genuine reconciliation is the goal. It may not be attained, but nonetheless, it is the goal.

In this book, I write about husbands leaving wives instead of mates leaving mates. Obviously, wives leave husbands, too. Just be aware that the parts are interchangeable. When I write about the reasons for husbands leaving wives, they are the same reasons for wives leaving husbands. And when I write about what a rejected wife needs to do, recognize that that is exactly what a rejected husband also needs to do. The principles work the same whether it is the husband or wife who wants to leave.

Whether you are personally in the midst of a separation, a counselor working with couples in this form of marital crisis, or a pastor trying to minister to a contemporary congregation, this book is for you. If you are only seeking to add to your insight or are painfully in need of direction in order to deal with your own marital turmoil, *When the One You Love Wants to Leave* offers both. With genuine reconciliation as a goal, I pray that this book will be helpful in your life.

This book is not just a book you sit down and read. Chances are, you are hurting when you read this and your journey through this book will take you through a roller coaster of emotions while at the same time helping you stabilize them. For this reason, there will be a series of questions and suggested readings that will help you clarify your thoughts on the chapter you just read. These questions will also help you understand how the previous chapter relates to your particular situation.

There are spaces for you to write the answers, or your thoughts, after each question. Writing these things down can be very helpful in the process of coming to terms with some of the issues. But there are two reasons why it may be more useful to write your answers down in a separate journal or notebook.

1. A separate notebook may give you a better sense of privacy which may help you be more honest in your thoughts, and

2. You may find that your answers and feelings change with time and circumstances. So, working through particular chapters more than once may be important for you in trying to resolve some of your thinking.

Part One

FIRST THINGS FIRST

1

"I'm Leaving"— A Crisis in the Marriage

Angela and Andy

From all appearances, Angela and Andy have an ideal marriage. But why shouldn't they? College sweethearts, they knew each other very well before marrying. Both were raised in stable and loving homes, they had similar backgrounds, and they shared the same values and religious beliefs. They seemed to be natural for each other. Angela and Andy represent that portion of Americans known as progressive conservatives. Andy's father is president of a Christian college, and all his siblings are in some form of church ministry. Andy was the principal of a Christian high school before going into a career in sales. Angela represents a blending of the traditional and the new. Balancing a career with the demands and the responsibilities of marriage and motherhood, she seems to have her act together. Actively involved in their local church, Angela and Andy seem to be an ideal example of the American work ethic.

Becky and Bill

After twenty years of marriage, Becky and Bill finally seem to have things going their way. Money has never been a problem. Owning their own business, they have worked together and built it into something of substance. Having just constructed a new home, they also own resort property that includes a condominium in Florida. What more could they want?

Even their relationship has improved. During the early years Bill had been peripheral in both his marital and family responsibilities. He would close up the business and then "go out with the boys," only to return home in the wee hours of the morning. Becky disapproved of his abandoning behavior but felt helpless to change it. Resuming church attendance a few years ago brought some dramatic changes in Bill's behavior. Although never an emotional sharer, he has at least ceased his more objectionable behavior and has become more involved as a husband and father. Season football tickets; flights to all of the away games; vacations together to the condo in Florida; home with the family after work; actively involved in the choir at church—Becky wonders if things could get any better than this.

Carol and Chuck

"A marriage made in heaven." "The ideal couple." "Made for each other." These familiar phrases probably fit some of the couples you know, but none of them applies to Carol and Chuck. The twelve years of their marriage were difficult from the start. There was always too little money, too little time, too little cooperation, and far too little caring. Between his job at the garage and the side work at home, Chuck has spent most of his time peering under the hoods of automobiles. But he likes it that way. As a true mechanic, cars have always been his first love. Chuck is a man of few words and, unfortunately for Carol, the few words he utters are not the ones she wants to hear. He sees his role as that of an order giver and Carol's as an order taker. While this worked in the earlier years of their marriage, the last few years have been marked by a distinct power struggle. Carol does not want to control Chuck, but neither does she want to be controlled by him. This sets a constant push-pull in motion. Taking a job, going out with the girls, and making time for herself have added to Carol's self-esteem. At the same time, Carol's newfound autonomy has prompted Chuck to withdraw more into himself. Carol feels more distant from him than ever before.

Diane and Dave

Diane and Dave live in an exclusive area of town. In fact, everything in their life is exclusive. Dave is a top business executive who has always achieved. Having power and position, he also commands a high salary. Their children attend the best private schools. As members of the country club, golf, tennis, fine dining, and splendid social gatherings are frequent occurrences. Diane spends most of her time running the home and keeping up with their social calendar. Dave is not much of a homebody, but he manages to be present when they entertain. In the earlier part of their marriage, Diane wanted more from Dave emotionally, but she gradually adapted her expectations and resigned herself to accepting Dave as he was. An affair Dave had eight years ago prompted a confrontation and almost ended the marriage, but when faced with an ultimatum, Dave chose to stay in the marriage and Diane accepted him back. That incident is basically forgotten now, even though its effects are still noticeable. Things have never quite been the same since. Although reasonably cooperative and cordial, the relationship has been sterile, and both seem to have resigned themselves to this form of existence.

All four of these marriages are different. One area of difference is in the history and development of the relationships. Each had a different beginning, each encountered a different set of problems, and each couple found a unique solution for their difficulties.

Another visible area of difference is in the interpersonal dynamics, or how the mates choose to relate to each other. For example, one couple is amiable and cooperative, whereas another is argumentative and resistant.

Differing socioeconomic characteristics are also evident. Not only is there a difference in the amount of education and money achieved and amassed, there is also a difference in the importance placed upon them.

I could continue to depict the differences among these four couples, but highlighting their distinctiveness is not my goal. What I really want to do is illuminate their *similarity*. What do all of these couples have in common? In each of these marriages, the husband has decided that he will leave the wife. And with the announcement of "I'm leaving," a *crisis* has come into the marriage.

Crisis brings commonality. Educational levels, financial resources, career accomplishments, social prominence, power, influence—all the things that serve to differentiate us from one another—fade from view and take a back seat when placed in the context of crisis. Somehow, these distinguishing characteristics seem far less important now. What becomes significant is the pain being experienced.

It is easier for us to think in terms of marital crisis than it is to think of *people* in crisis. It is less alarming, so we don't become as upset and uncomfortable. After all, marriages are institutions, abstract things that we can stay emotionally disengaged from. People, on the other hand, are flesh and blood. When people are in crisis, they hurt . . . they cry . . . they agonize. They don't eat, they don't sleep, they don't think straight, and they aren't much fun to be around. Rich or poor, educated or not, it makes little difference—people in crisis all tend to behave the same. They share the same pain, and for a while, that is all that seems to matter. What they now have in common far outweighs what they do not.

16

It is because there is such commonality in crisis that I can write this book, for with crisis and pain and commonality comes *predictability*. There is predictability in the pain experienced by an individual in crisis. There is also predictability in the courses of action followed by a couple in separation. The fact that there is predictability in personal crisis allows for intervention while giving us room for hope.

Rejectors and Rejectees

Why is marital separation so traumatic? Why is the departure of a husband so upsetting? There are a number of factors that contribute to the disruptive nature of separation. First, there are the purely logistical adjustments required by such a move. For example, there are now two residences to be maintained instead of one. With the additional living arrangements comes extra expense. Money issues are more complicated with separation, as are any tasks that had previously been cooperative ventures: child rearing, household responsibilities, and so forth.

A second factor contributing to the upset of separation is the general state of confusion that surrounds the relationship's future.

- Does his leaving mean we're going to get a divorce?
- He says he wants a divorce, but does he really mean it?
- He says he doesn't want a divorce. He only needs some time to think. What does that mean?
- How much time does he want? What am I to do while he's thinking?

These are common thoughts for wives who have been left by their husbands. Most divorces are preceded by a period of separation, but not all separations will end in divorce; hence the confusion. "Where is this relationship headed?" Along with the confusion prompted by this question comes high anxiety.

The final contributing factor to upset, and possibly the most significant, is the fact that humans are emotional beings. We like to think of ourselves as being rational or thinking beings, and we basically are. In fact, it's our high level of cognitive capability that separates us from other creations. Yet we tend to give ourselves too much credit and think of ourselves as being far more rational than we really are. In reality, we are rational *and* emotional, and sometimes our emotional selves overrule our rational selves.

When a couple separates, they do not simply and rationally move apart. There has been too much investment in each other's lives for separation to come this easily. Much like the bonding that takes place between a parent and a child, mates become emotionally attached to each other. The severing of these bonds is always accompanied by emotional pain, and no amount of rationalization will totally relieve it.

So emotional upset should come as no surprise during a separation. Yet, who fares the worse? Will the husband experience more emotional pain, or will the wife? How people fare in times of separation seems to be contingent upon a number of factors. There is some research to suggest that, all things being equal, women will have more difficulty with separation than men, so the degree of upset will be in part determined by the sex of the individual. Another important factor seems to be the level of emotional well-being or mental stability possessed by the individual prior to the crisis. Men and women who are emotionally healthy will handle separation better than those who are less healthy. A third factor influencing the degree of upset is the reason for the husband's departure. Although the reasons husbands leave will be discussed thoroughly in the next chapter, suffice it to say at this point that some reasons for departure are more traumatic than others.

Even though these are all important factors in determining who fares worse emotionally, the most significant factor seems to be who leaves whom. Whenever a mate wants to leave a marriage, two roles are assumed: one mate becomes the *rejector* and the other the *rejectee*. The rejector is the one who wants to leave; the rejectee is the one who is left. Of the two roles, the rejectee always fares worse.

A rejected wife experiences myriad thoughts and emotions; one of the more plaguing of these is guilt. She readily accepts blame for the separation. Whether her husband leaves for another woman or out of frustration from an unsatisfying relationship, the rejected wife believes she is at fault. She is the rejected one, she is the one who did not measure up. The relationship has failed, and so has she. If she only had tried harder . . . had done things better . . . had been more of what he needed . . . he would not have left. At least, this is what she thinks. And with this line of reasoning comes an overwhelming sense of guilt that haunts her day and night.

The rejected wife also experiences the pain of abandonment. She is left alone at a time when she desires solitude the least, and this aloneness is unbearable. The rejecting husband is far better prepared for the separation. He has the other woman, or desires the time apart, or has made plans for his future, all of which enable him to make the break with less difficulty. His wife—the rejectee—has none of these. She is unprepared. And being unprepared, her life is thrown into chaos. It is no surprise, therefore, that rejectees always fare the worse in separation.

Readiness

Emily and Ed had been separated for two months when they came to see me. I talked with them together at this first meeting. I asked each to tell me why they were here at this time and what they wanted to see happen. It quickly became evident that their motivation and desires were quite different. Emily spoke first. Anxious and on the verge of crying, she stated that her purpose was to save their marriage. "I want Ed to move back home and to try and work out our problems." She then went on to recount some of their six-year marital history, taking great pains to enumerate her wifely failures and shortcomings. Apologetic and remorseful, she was pleading for another chance at building the relationship.

Ed showed little sign of being emotionally swayed by Emily's words. He said he was at the session because of coercion. Preceded by constant pressure from Emily, a friend "finally talked me into it." However, Ed made it quite clear that his presence was not of his own choosing. "I tried to talk with Emily about my dissatisfactions throughout most of our marriage. She wouldn't listen. I finally got tired of the whole mess and said I wanted out. Now she's ready to 'work on things.' Well, it's too late. I have no interest in either Emily or the marriage. I'm not mad. I just want out."

During a marital separation, some things are constructive and right to do and others are not. Forcing a separating couple like Emily and Ed into traditional marriage counseling should definitely be avoided.

It is a natural response on the part of concerned friends and family members to encourage a separating couple to enter marital counseling. These concerned others genuinely care about the couple and do not want to see another marriage become a statistic. Unfortunately, this kind of help doesn't bring the desired results.

Traditional marriage counseling involves two mates who are intent on working on the relationship. Although the level of commitment may vary, there has to be some degree of desire on the part of *both* partners for this form of intervention to be effective. With Emily and Ed, the willingness to work on restoring the relationship was present in Emily but missing in Ed. If help had been sought before Ed had become emotionally distant, something might have been done to change the direction of the marriage. There may even be a time in the future when traditional marriage counseling can help Emily and Ed. If Ed changes his mind and decides that Emily and the relationship are both worth pursuing, conjoint intervention can begin. But for now, any efforts along this line are only counterproductive. If anything, they add to the problem instead of helping it. Pressuring a departing husband into working on his marriage only agitates an already tense situation.

The key to understanding the kind of intervention needed during separation is tied to the issue of readiness. For intervention of any kind to be effective, it must be consistent with what the mates are *ready* to do. For a couple like Emily and Ed, and almost all others who are separating, there is little readiness for traditional marital counseling.

The departing husband is leaving for a reason. As we will see later, it could be for any number of reasons. Still, he has made a decision, and for one reason or another, he has chosen to leave his wife. Before he will be ready to reconcile with her and truly work on the marriage, he must resolve whatever it is that has motivated him to leave. What is he pursuing outside of his marriage? Regardless of what this may be, until this motivation for leaving is resolved, he simply will not be ready to work on his marriage.

First Things First

My philosophy in working with separation is summarized by the statement "first things first." You can't deal with the marriage until whatever precipitated the husband's departure is resolved. You must deal with the separation before you can deal with the marriage.

Poor communication, insensitivity, lack of respect, failure to invest time and energy into the relationship—these cause marital problems, but they do not cause husbands to leave. They will eventually need to be corrected if the marriage is to grow, but now is not the time to work on them. You must first deal with the husband's reason for leaving.

Once this reason for leaving is successfully resolved, there may be an opportunity to deal with the marital relationship, but not before.

What needs to happen to make a husband ready to work on the marriage? It seems that readiness is closely related to the reason he left. As we better understand exactly why a husband leaves, we can see more clearly what needs to happen before he returns and what the wife can do to help this occur. With this in mind, I want to turn our attention to the primary reasons husbands leave their wives.

Study Questions

1. If both you and your spouse share anything at this juncture, it is probably the commonality of pain. Describe your feelings of pain.

2. What pain do you think your spouse is feeling?

3. Identify the issues that have become more complicated and how they have become complicated since the separation or the declaration of the need for separation.
   - children
   - finances
   - home
   - church
   - friends
   - other

4. Would you describe yourself as the *rejectee* or the *rejector*?

5. If you are the rejector, have you had any of the following thoughts or feelings? Elaborate on these:
   - guilt
   - not measuring up
   - feeling abandoned
   - other

Your Response

_____

_____

_____

_____

_____

_____

_____

_____

_____

_____

_____

_____

_____

_____

_____

_____

_____

_____

_____

2

Why Husbands Leave

What prompts a man, after years of seeming commitment to a relationship within marriage, to cast aside such a significant part of his life for something altogether new and different?

Contrary to the belief of many abandoned wives, it is *not* because these men are possessed, have suddenly gone crazy, or are under the influence of mind-altering drugs. Realistically, most husbands who find themselves in the role of rejector are normal, ordinary men.

Even though some husbands are so deviant—so irresponsible, so unreliable, so unstable, or so "in need of the hunt"—as to be accurately labeled pathological, the majority are not. Unless we wish to label the vast majority of our population as pathological, we have to abandon this perspective and view these men as they really are—ordinary men wanting out of their current relationships. But still, the establishing of this fact does not tell us *why* they leave.

When husbands want to leave wives, they give all sorts of reasons and excuses. They blame, they apologize, they accuse, they justify. Regardless of what they say, all rejectors can be placed into one of three categories. Husbands who leave wives are either *pulled* out, *pushed* out, or *put* out.

The *Pulled* Out

Husbands who are pulled out of a marriage leave for other women. These are the affairs. In situations like these, the emotional pull placed upon the husband's heartstrings is far greater from without the relationship than it is from within.

Gloria's separation was an example of this form of departure. After thirteen years of marriage, Glen came home from work one day and announced he was leaving. What he once felt for Gloria was gone; he now loved Mandy, a co-worker at the office.

Gloria was shocked and surprised. I asked if Glen had given any prior indications that he was seeing someone else or if he had seemed dissatisfied with the marriage. As she thought back over the previous year, she could recall a few changes in his behavior. Glen had seemed to be more emotionally distant, and he had less interest in sex, but he had also been working harder. She had attributed these changes to his longer hours at the office. There were no glaring indications that anything was wrong. Glen had voiced no complaints regarding the relationship, and family life seemed to continue as usual. To Gloria, the announcement was a total surprise.

Not all wives are as surprised as Gloria. While some are more suspicious than others, the lack of surprise is generally more closely related to the behavior of the husband than it is to the suspiciousness of the wife. Some men are just poor at deception. They either make numerous significant changes in their behavior patterns or fail to cover for themselves. I know of one instance where a husband of fifteen years suddenly acquired a completely new wardrobe, bought a sports car, dyed his hair, began using cologne, and changed from wearing regular underwear to skimpy bikini briefs. All these changes occurred in a span of three months and accompanied longer hours at work and increased time away from home. An affair might not be the only explanation for these sudden changes, but deviation of this magnitude from his former patterns of behavior could cause a wife to wonder.

Other men reduce the potential for surprise by failing to cover themselves. They are careless: lipstick on the collar of a shirt, the scent of perfume on their clothing, not being where they said they would be. Many a husband has been foiled by a motel receipt or an unexplainable credit-card slip carelessly left and accidentally detected.

But for Gloria, this was not the case. Glen had been careful; his indiscretion had been less than obvious. For Gloria, the announcement came as a total surprise. "I pleaded with Glen to stay. I told him we could work it out. I asked him to think of the children. I was a hysterical wreck. None of it fazed him. He just calmly packed his bags and left."

Men who leave marriages for other women share much in common with one another. In fact, as we shall see, each of these three categories—the pulled out, the pushed out, and the put out—have characteristics that uniquely define the men who comprise them. Husbands who are pulled out share the following characteristics.

Frequency

Men more frequently leave their wives for other women than for any other single reason. It would be difficult to cite an exact statistic, but with the soaring rate of infidelity currently found within American marriages, the fact that men more often leave wives for other women comes as no surprise.

Degree of Resolve

Husbands who are pulled out of marriages tend to be resolute about their decision. While Gloria was pleading and near hysterics, Glen was methodically packing his bags. His mind was made up; he would not be swayed.

Many people have difficulty understanding how a husband could be so resolute. It shocks them. How could he be so callous? How could he do this? The answer is simple: He is being controlled by his emotional system.

People in general, especially those within the conservative church community, fail to have a healthy respect for the power of human emotions. We prefer to see mankind as totally rational and fully capable of doing the right thing. We like to think that telling a man what he "should," "ought," or "must" do is all that's necessary. As far as emotionality goes, I'm afraid we tend to have our heads in the sand. The influence of emotions is powerful, and failing to respect this power is dangerous. The husband who is involved in an affair is caught up in the height of emotion. In his mind, he loves this other woman. It feels so good that he has no doubts about what he must do.

Urgency

A third distinguishing characteristic of husbands who are pulled out of marriage is that they are more likely to seek an immediate divorce. This is not to say that they will always ask for one. However, of those husbands who leave wives, these men, more than the others, feel ready to finalize their decision.

I believe this urgency in seeking a divorce is directly related to their reasons for leaving. Their strong emotional tie to the other woman makes these husbands resolute in the decision to leave. This being the case, why should they wait around and belabor the issue?

"The marriage is dead. Let's get on with the living. Why waste time? I'm not going to change my mind." With this line of reasoning, husbands frequently seek as quick a divorce as possible.

How He Fares Emotionally

Another distinguishing characteristic has to do with how the departing husband fares emotionally. Of the three categories of rejectors, those pulled out of marriage fare the best and experience the least emotional difficulty.

The reason for their calmness is fairly obvious: They are not leaving an unsatisfactory marriage to begin a solitary existence. They are just leaving one relationship for another. Besides, they believe they are in love. These rejectors are the least bothered by confusion and plaguing feelings of loneliness, so it is only natural that their initial adjustment to the separation will be fairly easy.

Of course the wives of these men suffer deeply. To be cast aside for another woman cuts more deeply than any other form of rejection.

Emotional Contradiction

A final characteristic deals with the level of emotional contradiction present in separations. The greatest contradiction between what a husband *says* and what he *does is* noted in this category. Husbands who are pulled out reportedly do not understand why their wives are so devastated. They coolly, calmly, and rationally assert that their wives should be less upset.

"You need to take hold of yourself. Why are you so upset? I'm doing the best thing. After all, you don't want to live with a man who does not love you. In the long run, I'm doing what is best for both of us. Why can't you just accept it and get over this thing?"

These husbands appear to be so noble, so strong, so rational, so above the normal human pitfall of emotions. Wrong! In actuality, they are as caught up in emotions as their rejected partners. Although a rational front is projected, this is only because they have largely severed their emotional attachments in one relationship and redirected them to another.

In reality, these husbands are operating totally on emotions. After all, it is their strong emotional pull toward someone else that prompted the marital crisis. Their emotional system is running at full tilt. Why else would they so drastically change their behavior and devastate the lives of those around them? They are doing this because they *feel* like doing it. They are emotionally engulfed by another woman, and it feels so good. Their supposed failure to understand the emotional reaction of their abandoned wives is only a tribute to the situational insensitivity of the moment, not only toward the turmoil of their mates, but to themselves as well. They simply do not perceive the great contradiction that exists in their lives.

The *Pushed* Out

Husbands who are pushed out of a marriage leave through frustration. They feel trapped and intruded upon. They crave space. They believe that remaining in the marriage would mean certain engulfment and smothering. It is either get out or perish.

It was unusual for me to see someone like Harold in my counseling practice, not so much because of his high socio-economic status, but because of his role in the marriage. He was the rejector, and it's usually the rejectee who comes looking for help.

Harold was the proverbial example of rags to riches. He was used to setting goals and achieving them. He wanted a college education and got one. He wanted to marry Helen and did. He wanted his dream house by thirty and financial security by thirty-five, both of which he achieved. He also wanted to retire from his business by age forty. He was now thirty-nine and one-half, and there was every indication that this retirement goal would also be reached. But he was not happy.

> If I were to be honest, I guess I've really been unhappy with my marriage for a number of years. I just never realized it. Approaching forty has caused me to do some heavy self-evaluation. It's not so much a mid-life crisis as much as it is reaching goals.
>
> All of my life has been planned around goals, and my ultimate dream has been to retire at age forty. I wanted to be so successful, so financially secure, that I could spend the rest of my life in a carefree existence. I wanted to spend my time traveling around the world with Helen and dabbling in any business deals that might interest me. Well, I'm thirty-nine and one-half. And the closer I get to forty, knowing that all of this is within reach, the more anxious and depressed I get. During the past year I have been forced to look seriously at my marriage. And what I've found scares me to death.
>
> Helen and I are two miserable, unhappy, and depressed people. We argue all the time now, and it's getting worse daily. We're totally different people. We have different goals, different desires, different outlooks in life. I could go on and on. My preoccupation with business is the only thing that has kept me sane throughout the past five years. The more I think about it, the more depressed I get. I've made up my mind. Retiring to spend more time with Helen would be sure hell. I've got to get out of the relationship and get some peace of mind.

Harold was so frustrated with his marriage that he wanted to leave his wife, and he did. Thinking about remaining in the marriage created so much emotional discomfort that it was finally easier to get out than stay in.

As is the case with husbands who are pulled out of marriages, men like Harold, who are pushed out, have characteristics that differentiate them from those who leave for other reasons.

Frequency

The first characteristic to be considered is frequency of occurrence. The number of husbands who leave their wives out of frustration lags far behind those who leave for other women. At least, this is my observation. Actual research in this area is fairly sparse. But throughout the years of my practice as a marriage counselor, the husbands who genuinely leave out of sheer frustration are in the minority.

Lest there be any confusion regarding this issue of frequency, I want to offer two points of clarification. I'm speaking of husbands who *genuinely* leave out of frustration. Husbands always leave for a reason, but sometimes the reason they give is not the true reason for leaving. It's not unusual for a man who is actually being pulled out to claim that he is being pushed out. Attempting to protect himself and the woman with whom he is involved, he simply states that he can no longer remain in the marriage.

I refer to these men as "false positives." While claiming to be one thing, they are actually another. Therefore, their claim is false. These "false positives" usually have weak rationales or justifications for wanting to leave. One wife caught in such a situation shared with me her confusion regarding her husband's inability to give a clear reason for leaving.

"I don't understand it. He just came in and said he was leaving. I asked him why. Was there anything I had done? He identified some minor things but nothing major enough to warrant breaking up a marriage. He said he couldn't explain his feelings. He just knew he had to get out. The more I asked, the more I got 'I don't know' in response. I'm totally confused."

Husbands who are truly pushed out do not arrive at this juncture impulsively; their decision to leave has been contemplated for some time. They have thought about it time and time again, and when asked why, their response is not "I don't know." They know why, and they state it. Just because a husband says he is leaving because of frustration does not make it a fact.

If truly pushed-out men are in the minority, does that mean marital dissatisfaction is also in the minority? I think this would be a faulty assumption. Marital dissatisfaction is fairly commonplace in our society, but so is complacency. For existing structures to be changed, there must be motivation—people have to be emotionally energized to uproot their lives. Many marriages, although failing in nature, will rock on as they are until something happens to create enough energy for change, whether in a positive or negative direction.

The men who are pulled out of relationships are dissatisfied and frustrated with their marriages, but it's the feelings they have for the other woman that give them the emotional energy to do something about their dissatisfaction. It just so happens that their manner of dealing with their dissatisfaction is to leave the marriage.

The same is true for pushed-out husbands. The emotional energy required to push someone out of a marriage is enormous—far more than that generated in the ordinary unsatisfactory marriage. This doesn't mean there are only a few unsatisfactory relationships. It only means that the level of frustration has not yet reached a point that provides enough motivation for the husband to change the present structure. When men become frustrated enough, they leave.

Precipitants

For the pulled-out husband, there is one and only one precipitant—another woman. For the pushed-out husband, there can be multiple precipitants.

For years the failing marriage has rocked on. Why is the frustration finally getting to a level that prompts change? It could be a mid-life crisis and the introspection that accompanies it. It could be a hidden affair that, even though now over and resolved, makes existing within a failing relationship unbearable. It could be the divorce of a close friend that prompts an evaluation of his own marital relationship. It could be a geographical move and the severing of old support networks. It could be the disruption brought about by extreme external crises. In short, it could be anything that makes the failing nature of the marriage overt and suddenly intolerable.

Degree of Resolve

Pushed-out husbands seem to be less resolute about their decision to leave than pulled-out husbands. Leaving is what they want to do, but there is always some confusion. Remember, they do not have the pull of waiting arms beckoning them to come out. Rather, they are fleeing an intolerable situation. Is it really that bad? Are things really going to be any better away from the marriage? Questions like these cause husbands to have nagging doubts about their decisions.

Urgency

Closely related to the resoluteness of their decision is their attitude about seeking an immediate divorce. A pushed-out husband is far more hesitant to seek an immediate dissolution of the marriage than his pulled-out counterpart. He thinks a divorce is what he wants, but he isn't certain. He doesn't want to make a mistake. Seeking a divorce is too big a step for him to take all at once. He doesn't want to burn his bridges until he is certain of his future, so he asks for "time to think" instead.

"I don't want a divorce . . . just time to think. I just need some space to myself. There's no one else in my life. I just don't know if I love you the way I used to. Just give me some time."

What he doesn't know is whether he can stand to be away. Is it really any better out there? So he hesitates.

How He Fares Emotionally

Pushed-out husbands experience a moderate degree of emotional difficulty. It is not difficult to figure out why this is the case. Remember, the pulled-out husband leaves for the other woman. He is immediately "connected." The pushed-out husband, on the other hand, has no other attachment. There is no one out there waiting to "fill him up." There is no immediate end result but space, and space, even though highly sought after, can sometimes be lonely. There may be an immediate sense of relief, but these husbands then have to deal with the aloneness that accompanies separation.

- Are things really any better?

- Where are all the unattached women who want an enduring companionship relationship?

- Where is the swinging singles life?

- Why is it I'm not satisfied with throwing myself totally into my work?

- Is there such a thing as having too much space?

Questions like these interfere with the relief of escape. These husbands have left one problem for another, and their adjustment is not always an easy one.

The *Put* Out

Husbands who are put out of a marriage are forced to leave. Unlike the other two categories of departing husbands, they may not want to leave, but continuous and repetitive acts of irresponsible behavior finally necessitate strong measures on the part of their more responsible and exasperated wives. Flagrantly abused, these wives finally get to the point of taking a stand. No more excuses. No more second chances. No more acquiescence. For their own sanity, and possibly for the well-being of the children, these wives finally *put* their husbands out.

Some would argue that this is really a matter of a wife leaving her husband rather than a husband leaving his wife. I can understand the confusion, yet I still believe it is the wife who is being left. In a very real, emotional sense, she is the rejectee. The separation is not something she wanted. In fact, it's something she has avoided for years. She has wanted a good and satisfying marriage. She has given; she has pleaded; she has begged. But time after time, she has been ignored.

Repeatedly, her pleas for a different life-style have been rejected. Maybe he rejected her pleas for a safe marriage and chose to offer abuse, whether physical or emotional. Maybe he rejected her pleas for monogamy and chose to have numerous relationships with other women. Or maybe he rejected her pleas for a dependence-free marriage and chose to devote himself to drugs or alcohol. How the story line is played out varies from marriage to marriage, but the variations make little difference. What's important is that the wife, whose pleas for a safe and sane relationship have been repeatedly rejected, is finally forced to take a stand. The cycle of destruction has to stop, and in order to take a stand, this rejectee puts her husband out of the marriage.

Irene represents a classic example of this form of separation. Her fourteen-year marriage had been anything but blissful. Isach was self-centered, insensitive, and controlling. The autonomy she enjoyed by having a career only fanned the flames under Isach's need to be in charge. He was constantly trying to bring Irene into line. Irene suggested repeatedly that they seek professional help, but Isach refused. When he was the angriest, he would hit her, and as time went on, Isach became more and more angry.

Still, Irene held on, clinging to the hope that they could pull their marriage together. At least she clung to that hope until an incident occurred that demanded she take a stand.

"Things had been getting worse, and I knew it. But I just kept hoping . . . hoping Isach would change . . . hoping he would go to counseling . . . hoping he would stop hitting me. Then one day, in the middle of an argument, my son burst into the room and shouted at Isach, 'I'm not going to let you hit my mother again!' He was going to fight his daddy. My twelve-year-old! That was all I could stand. I couldn't let things go on anymore. I had to take control. So I did."

Irene was forced to take a stand, so she put Isach out of the marriage. Yes, she initiated it, but emotionally she was the rejectee. This was not what she wanted, and it wasn't easy. As a rejectee, her experience during this time of separation was much the same as any other woman who is left by her husband.

Men who are put out of their marriages have characteristics uniquely differentiating them from those who leave for other reasons.

Frequency

The number of husbands who are put out of marriages is relatively small, compared to the other categories, but this isn't because irresponsible husbands are a rare occurrence. In actuality, many men are irresponsible. The fact that there are as few husbands put out of marriages as there are is attributable to the enduring nature of their wives.

Marriages of this type take on a very cooperative flavor, with two roles being played. The husband's role is to be irresponsible; the wife's role is to put up with his irresponsibility. In essence, the wives in marriages of this type have a real part in maintaining their husbands' behavior. Although they formally state that they disapprove of what their husbands are doing, their willingness to allow it to go on grants these men informal permission to continue as they please. Without this permission, it is less likely that it would persist.

Why these wives willingly play their role is difficult to say. Some feel trapped. "What else could I do? I've got three kids and no means of support other than what my husband gives me. I have no other choice."

Others claim that they are compelled by love for their husbands. "No matter what he does, I can't get past the fact that I love him. I know he really loves me too . . . in his own way. I don't know what I'd do if I couldn't be near him."

Still others believe it is their lot in life to submit to their husbands' desires and demands and accept their irresponsible behavior. "I am his wife. He is the head of the house. I may not like what he does, but he is still the boss. That's the way it is meant to be."

The reasons these wives continue to behave as they do really make little difference; the end result is the same. These wives help their husbands to be irresponsible, and some of them are content to do so forever.

Precipitants

The reasons for putting a husband out of a relationship can be multiple. One such precipitant is addiction to drugs and alcohol. Life with a man whose very reason for existence is to obtain and use these substances is pure torture. Under their influence, he sacrifices job and family. The unpredictability of his behavior destroys a marriage.

Another precipitant is physical abuse. Media attention focusing on family violence has made us painfully aware of the epidemic proportion of this problem. Coupled with the problem of physical abuse is the precipitant of emotional abuse. Although the scars are less obvious to the eye, they are present, just the same, and constant berating by an emotionally abusive husband takes a heavy toll.

Flagrant affairs, habitual lying, excessive control, addictive gambling . . . the list goes on and on. In fact, you can probably add some to my list. As you can see, irresponsibility can be played out in many ways.

Nature of Precipitants

The precipitants may be multiple, but they all share four things in common. First, they are patterns, not isolated behaviors. As a therapist I know that if I observe anyone for a long enough period of time, I might witness almost any conceivable form of behavior. Knowing this, I am seldom alarmed with anything that I see on a one-time basis. If I begin to see certain behaviors on a repetitive basis, however, I become concerned. When dealing with the kinds of irresponsible precipitants that prompt wives to put husbands out of marriages, we are never dealing with isolated occurrences. We are always dealing with patterns—repetitive occurrences of the same behavior. And it is this frequency that eventually prompts action.

A second commonality is that the husband's irresponsible behavior is always self-seeking. He selfishly pursues his own needs or interests at the expense of those around him. No one else seems to matter. At least they matter less than he does.

A third characteristic of the husband's irresponsible behavior is that it is *deviant,* as opposed to merely being *different.* Mates can have differences. For example, my wife is a morning person, whereas I am a night person. This requires adjustments on both of our parts. But being either a morning person or a night person is not considered deviant—it is only different. Irresponsible behavior is deviant: It is unacceptable behavior in any context, including marriage.

I recently saw a woman whose husband constantly berated her because she refused to accept his "differences." "You ought to accept me as I am. You're my wife. If you were as Christian as you say you are, you wouldn't give me a hard time for being the way that I am. We just don't like the same things."

The "difference" he was referring to was that he liked to smoke marijuana. From his perspective, she was being unreasonable for not allowing him to do so. But to her, this was deviant and totally unacceptable behavior.

Finally, irresponsible behavior is always destructive, sometimes for the husband himself. Often it is destructive for his wife, but it's always destructive for the relationship. Even in instances where mates stay together, the marriage fails.

Urgency

Husbands who are put out of marriages are the least likely to seek an immediate divorce. In fact, they will vehemently resist one if it is sought by their wives. These husbands want to stay married and move back home, but they don't want to see things changed.

The immediate goal of put-out husbands is to get things

back to the way they were, not to change. They believe that if they can just get back into the house, their wives will "fall back in line" and it will soon be business as usual. There are two primary tactics utilized by these husbands to get back home. The first is false acquiescence, where they are immediately remorseful. They willingly confess their wrongdoing and promise to change. Unfortunately, with men who have a history of repetitive irresponsibility, these promises to change are of little value. Although oftentimes they are convincing ploys, they are offered only as a manipulation. Remember, their goal is to get back home.

The other primary tactic for getting back home is the use of force. This may only be in the form of threats and intimidation, but it is not unusual for these men to be very "active" in their efforts to "get things back to the way they were." They are desperate. They need to control. And as long as they are out of the home, they are out of control.

Desperate situations call for desperate measures, so they harass; they show up unannounced and create disturbances; they become violent; they lie to friends and relatives, creating a difficult living situation for their wives; they withhold financial support; they have friends and well-meaning others apply pressure on their wives to "take the husband back" . . . the list goes on and on. In short, they do whatever it takes to get back home. Once home, their goal becomes to reinstate the cycle of irresponsibility.

How He Fares Emotionally

Of the three types of men who leave wives, husbands who are put out fare the worst emotionally. Quite simply, they do not want to be out of the home.

Men who are irresponsible and repeatedly perform deviant and/or abusive behavior are usually quite dependent upon their wives for emotional support. Even though they often project a macho bravado, these men are seldom self-reliant. Put out of the marriage, they find the aloneness of separation to be unbearable and become depressed and despondent. And it is this emotional devastation, coupled with their need to control, that motivates them to get back home at any cost.

Summary of Attitudes

Men who are pulled out of marriage believe: "I have definitely found something better."

Men who are pushed out offer a less resolute attitude: "There has to be something better."

Those husbands who are put out of the marriage believe: "I have to get back at any cost."

There are three different motivations for leaving, three different attitudes at the time of departure, and three different resolutions that must occur before the marriage can be restored. For the husband who is being *pulled* out, the pull has to end. If and when his attitude that "there is something better" dissolves, the possibility for working toward reconciliation presents itself. For the husband who is *pushed* out, the possibility of reconciliation accompanies the deterioration of his fantasy that things are naturally better outside the marriage. With the realization that the grass isn't always greener comes motivation to reinvest in the marriage. And for the husband who is put out, work toward restoration can begin only when he demonstrates genuine change in his behavior.

Even though the motivations and resolutions of the husbands are greatly different, the actions that need to be taken by their abandoned wives are the same. Regardless of why her husband leaves, a rejected wife has one—and only one—response that is best for her and the possible restoration of the marital relationship.

Study Questions

1. If you are the rejectee, indentify the category your spouse fits in as the rejector. Using the "pulled out," "pushed out," and "put out" descriptions in this chapter, list the reasons why each category does or does not represent your particular situation.

   - "Pulled out"
   - "Pushed out"
   - "Put out"

2. Once you have identified whether your spouse was "pulled out," "pushed out," or "put out," elaborate on the following:

   - Was there a precipitant, or something that caused the action?

   - How firm is the resolve your spouse has toward the separation?

   - Is there an urgency to your spouse's desire for divorce or has he expressed a desire for reconciliation?

   - How do you think your spouse fares emotionally?

Your Response

3

What to Do

My husband is leaving me for another woman. What should I do?

My husband is tired of our relationship. Out of frustration, he is leaving me. What am I to do?

I can't stand it any longer. My husband is so irresponsible. Things have to change. I have asked him to leave. Now, what should I do?

What should a wife do? When a husband leaves, whether he is pulled out, pushed out, or put out, are some actions better than others? Is there a preferred course of action?

When your husband leaves, there are three options available to you. You can: immediately divorce him; pursue him; or let him go.

Far too often, we *react* emotionally instead of *acting* rationally. This can get us into trouble. When making a decision about how to respond to a departing husband, you should not be controlled by your emotions and do what feels good. Rather, you need to determine exactly what your *goal is* for the relationship. What do you want to see happen? Do you want the marriage to end? Do you want it to continue along in a confused state? Or do you want an opportunity for reconciliation? Once your goal is identified, a course of action is automatically dictated. It may not be what you feel like doing. It may not be what you want to do. But it will be the course of action that is best for you to follow. Let's look at the three options available to you and the goal of each.

Immediately Divorce Him

From a purely rational point of view, the consequence of divorce—thus its goal—is the dissolution of the relationship. The marriage ends. Some wives take a fairly strong "divorce the sucker" attitude and respond to a husband who has been pulled out of the relationship with immediate legal action. They feel hurt, embarrassed, and angry. They may want to get even. "I'll show you!" They may be concerned about their image. "All my friends know what he's doing. I have my pride." They may even think it is their responsibility to divorce him. "I have biblical grounds. I'm supposed to divorce him."

Wives whose husbands are pushed out of the marriage have many of the same thoughts and feelings. Although they are usually a little less certain regarding the biblical grounds, they reactively take the position, "If he doesn't want me, then I certainly don't want him." This line of reasoning is immediately followed by legal action.

Some of the wives in put-out situations are also ready to divorce their husbands. Their readiness stems from feelings of hopelessness. After years of tolerating a husband's continued irresponsibility, it seems that the step from finally putting him out to filing for divorce is a short one. As one weary and beleaguered wife remarked to me: "He's never going to change. He's always *been* this way . . . and he'll always *be* this way. I'm only fooling myself to think things will ever be any different. With as much trouble as I've had to get to this point, I might as well follow through and end it all right now."

I understand the many and varied feelings that surround the departure of a husband. Furthermore, I realize that there are occasions when there seems to be no other realistic answer. Yet I do not like to see divorce exercised as an immediate first choice. It is so final. To respond to a husband who has left the marriage by immediately filing for divorce is to assert the goal of marital dissolution. You are stating that your goal for the marriage is that it should end. There is little chance for reconciliation in this decision, and it is my belief that, as Christians, reconciliation should always be our first goal. Divorce may end up being the ultimate choice, but it rarely needs to be the first.

Pursue Him

Pursuing a husband who has left the marriage is the most frequent response. It's natural behavior for a rejected mate. She wants him back at any cost. She cries, she begs, she pleads. "Think of the children." "How can you hurt me this way?" "I will be a better wife . . . just give me another chance." Pursuing wives accept all blame and total responsibility for the marital failure. They are loving though rejected. They are forgiving though there is no sign of remorse. In short, they are hanging on.

Seldom does pursuing result in the return of the departed husband. With some degree of embarrassment, most of the rejected wives who come to me for counseling report that they have already tried it, to no avail. Even when it does bring the husband back, the marriage does not heal. It only proceeds in a precarious fashion until a later event precipitates another crisis.

The reality of this situation is best illustrated by the case of Jean. When Jean and Dave came to my office, they had already been separated for three weeks. It seemed to be a fairly classic pulled-out situation, although Dave was disguising this by reporting that he was pushed out. Dave stated that he wanted the marriage to work but he was not certain it could. I suspect that he was more interested in getting his wife connected with a counselor to help her with her emotional upset than he was in any genuine attempt to save their marriage. At any rate, he declined the offer to be involved in further counseling. "Work with Jean. She's the one who is upset. I'm not sure what I want to do." As I worked with Jean, I found that this was the second separation in their twenty-year marital history. The first had occurred eight years earlier and was surrounded with strikingly similar circumstances.

I remember Dave's leaving me eight years ago as if it were yesterday. He said he had been unhappy throughout most of the marriage. He just hadn't made a big deal out of it. But he couldn't stand it any longer. He wanted out. So he rented an apartment and moved.

I was devastated. I did everything possible to try and get him to move back. I learned that he was seeing another woman. This only made me more frantic. I behaved then much the same way I'm behaving now. It didn't seem to do anything but drive him further away.

Finally, after four months of pleading, he decided to move back. It was kind of a sudden decision. One moment he wouldn't hear of it and the next—there he. was. I'm not sure why he decided to come back. I only know I was so relieved.

But my sense of relief did not last long. I don't know what it was, but things were different. After a while, I began to feel resentful. He was back . . . and I had begged him to return . . . but now I was angry.

Who did he think he was? He walked out on me with no explanation other than I was a terrible wife. And then he just as suddenly walked back into the marriage. There was no explanation, no apology, no nothing. We just continued as if the previous four months had never existed. I could never get close to him after that.

There was always something between us. The marriage just coolly "rocked on."

The goal of pursuing is to keep a marriage intact, keeping mates together at any cost. As the case of Jean and Dave illustrates, however, being intact and being *reconciled* are greatly different things. Only the latter offers a constructive future for the relationship.

Most of us in conservative Christendom are enamored with the concept of "intactness." It is believed that as long as a couple stays together, everything is okay; therefore, our goal is simply to keep people together. If they separate, our goal remains the same: get them back together.

As we follow Jesus through the New Testament, we find that His goal was not intactness. At least, that was not His primary goal. If it was a goal at all, it was only as a by-product of reconciliation. Jesus preached reconciliation, and He also acted it out. There are repeated instances where He criticized the Pharisees for their appearance of righteousness when in fact their true spiritual lives resembled "dead men's bones" in whited sepulchers (*see* Matthew 23:27). He demanded genuine spiritual reconciliation and would not settle for a sham substitute. Were His goal simply the appearance of unity—if He valued intactness above everything else—He would have compromised His response to the rich young ruler in order to keep him from going away sorrowfully *(see* Matthew 19:16-22). But again, intactness was not His primary goal. Jesus wanted relationships to be intact, but He knew that true togetherness was the by-product of a reconciled life and not the outward appearance of unity.

For reconciliation to occur in a marriage, both mates have to be actively, genuinely involved. There needs to be a forgiver and a forgivee. Remorsefully, a husband seeks forgiveness.

Graciously, a wife extends it. This constitutes reconciliation, and reconciliation allows for healing and restoration. It may be that each mate will have occasion to play both roles, having opportunity not only to forgive but also to be forgiven. Regardless, however, reconciliation is a far richer experience than the mere return of a husband, sauntering back to the wife he had left, fully intending an unobstructed resumption of "things as they were."

You may think that you want to see your marriage restored and justify your willingness to pursue your husband in an effort to reach this goal. However, pursuing seldom brings a husband back. It generally only succeeds in pushing him farther away. Even in those instances where he does come home, it is rarely a healthy return with genuine remorse. He seldom willingly takes responsibility for his role in the marital failure. Rather, he returns on his own terms. "I'm back. I don't want to hear anything about it. I don't want to talk about it. Let's just go on as if nothing ever happened."

Pursuing a husband only perpetuates marital confusion. If the price for keeping a marriage intact is to fail to deal with the relationship, then the cost is too high. The example offered by Jean and Dave illustrates this for us. Without genuine reconciliation, the marriage will only continue to fail.

Let Him Go

If immediately divorcing a husband ends the relationship and pursuing him only interferes with genuine reconciliation, what's a wife to do? What response works toward healthy restoration of the marriage and enhances the emotional stability of the rejected wife? Simply stated, when your husband wants to leave, you should let him go. By this, I mean that you ought to back off and give him some rope. That's not to say that you give him an immediate divorce. You do give him some time to come around. "If it's space you want, it's space you've got."

Letting your husband go is not the easiest thing to do. In fact, it is probably the most difficult of the three options. Divorcing him or pursuing him are much simpler. They're also what you most generally feel like doing. However, if you are going to decide what to do on the basis of your desired outcome for the relationship, and not necessarily according to how you feel, this is the appropriate action. *The goal of letting your husband go is to get him back.*

Backing off and letting your husband go works toward reconciliation in two ways. First, it gives your husband an opportunity to resolve whatever motivated him to leave in the first place. This is illustrated in the diagram on the following page.

Emotionally, he is swinging out of the marriage. You want him to swing in, but he won't do this until he resolves whatever it is that has prompted his swing out. Was it another woman? Letting him go will force him to deal with reality. The people involved in affairs are bigger than life; they are illusions. The sneaking around and the aura of forbidden fruit only add to the mystique. This is all eliminated when the affair is out in the open and you let him go. Now things are seen as they really are. There are no knights in shining armor, and there are no pure maidens, either. If the illusion is replaced with reality, the affair may dissolve. Without that pulling him out, your husband may be willing to swing back into the marriage.

The same principle holds true for the husband who is pushed out. He, too, must resolve his motivation for leaving. Primarily, he left in search of greener pastures that are frequently only illusions. Giving him some space and time may lead to his discovering that greener pastures, at least as he envisioned them, are only a myth. If this occurs, he may be ready to swing back into the marriage.

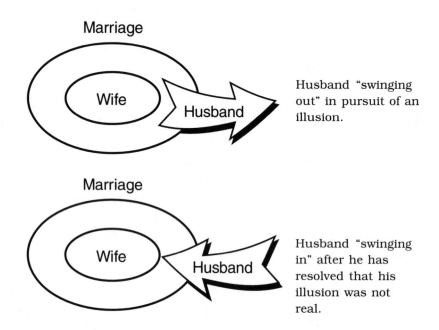

Husband "swinging out" in pursuit of an illusion.

Husband "swinging in" after he has resolved that his illusion was not real.

The second way letting your husband go works toward reconciliation is that it removes his comfort zone. Your pursuing him gives him a sense of security and comfort. Sure, he's out there doing his thing, but you're still there, eagerly waiting for his return. He knows he can return with no questions asked, on his terms. When you let him go, you take this security away. He can no longer have his cake and eat it, too. You force him to assume responsibility for what he is doing and create a crisis for him. Controlling your behavior in this manner and creating this crisis is the only real power you have left in the relationship. He is forced to experience the separation and what it means to be alone. His anxiety rises. Good! He needs to face this reality and feel the discomfort. All of this aids in his decision making. With the comfort zone removed, he is more apt to decide to swing in than if the comfort zone remains in place.

Letting him go is not an easy task. As one wife put it, "Until a decision is made, it's like walking on Jell-O. Life is never stable." This isn't a foolproof means of getting your husband back, but when you consider the alternatives, it does appear to be the best option available.

How to Let Your Husband Go

Letting your husband go is not an easy task, but it is achievable. Part of what interferes with your accomplishing this feat is not knowing exactly what to do. When it comes to letting your husband go, I have identified six steps that need to be taken. Your ultimate success will largely be determined by how well you perform each of these steps.

Take a Stand

Taking a stand requires a decision to do so and making a statement to that effect. This statement is very important. In therapy, I refer to this as a *declaration. You* are declaring exactly what you will do, and what you won't.

You can use your own words to compose the declaration. It need not be lengthy. However, it should encompass the following four themes:

- Reaffirm your love for your husband.
- State your genuine concern for the marriage and your desire that it be continued.
- State your willingness to give him some time to make a decision regarding whether he wishes to remain in the marriage.
- State that your decision to give him some space is time limited. You will not wait forever.

Making this kind of statement demonstrates strength to your husband, a far different image than that presented by the pursuing wife. This declaration may be spoken or written. Do whatever is easiest for you. What is important to remember, however, is that it needs to be largely devoid of angry attacks or pleading. A cool, calm, collected, matter-of-fact demeanor is what you're striving to project. Once you have made your declaration, do not constantly restate it. This would only become another form of pursuing behavior. You made your statement; now let it lie. The ball is in his court.

Taking a stand in this manner helps you gain some control of your emotions. Part of this calming comes from the fact that you now have direction: You have a course of action to follow, instead of wondering what is the right thing to do. You are also aided by the fact that you are making a decision about the future of your relationship. You are deciding not to decide. Rather than having to make a decision on whether to stay in the marriage or not, you are choosing to put this off for a definite period and allow time to work for you. Deciding not to decide places this issue on the back burner and takes the pressure off. You have identified a time in the future when you will reconsider the problem, although you have not informed your husband of the exact time frame. At that distant time, you will re-evaluate your data. For now, you can rest assured that the situation will be dealt with. It will not rock on indefinitely.

Back Off

After declaring that you are going to give your husband space, do it. Back off. Do not pursue him, either out of neediness or anger. Have no contact with him other than out of necessity. Stop the phone calls and any other attempts to see him in person. You may have to resist urges to restate your declaration and explain yourself to him. Contact needs to be restricted to essential business only. When you do have unavoidable contact with your husband, you need to project a cool, calm, well-controlled image.

It is not unusual to find that once you stop making frequent and impassioned phone calls to your husband, he will begin to call you. Sometimes he will use business as an excuse or say he's just calling to see how you are doing. This maintains his comfort zone. Even though you tried to sever it, he is maintaining an emotional connection. If this occurs, you need to ask him not to call except for legitimate business, and this can generally be conducted at one specific time during the week. If he persists, say that talking with him is emotionally difficult for you. There is no doubt in your mind that you will survive the experience, but for now, it is not in your best interest to have frequent contact with him. Tell him that if he persists, you will have no alternative but to hang up the telephone when he calls. Of course, be cool, calm, and collected. Backing off is aimed at giving you the greatest opportunity for emotional calmness while enhancing your husband's discomfort.

Structure the Separation

You need to define the rules and roles of this separation. For instance, sometimes husbands want to leave but don't. One client told me how she put up with years of verbal abuse from her husband. He said he didn't love her. The only reason he stayed was the children, although he was not very active in his parental role, either. He regretted the day he married . . . she was such a poor wife . . . he ought to leave. But he didn't. He just stayed around and kept pounding his wife's self-esteem right into the ground.

At other times, husbands *act* as if they have already left when they haven't. One wife shared with me that for years her husband would stay out all night and flagrantly speak of all the women he was involved with. In situations like these, clarifying the situation may involve helping the husbands along to an actual separation.

In most instances where structuring is required, the actual separation has already taken place. In these situations, structuring refers to the clarification of the rules regarding how you will relate during this time. This usually involves two areas: living arrangements and personal contact. When it comes to living arrangements, decisions need to be made regarding his coming and going. Will he be allowed to drop in as he pleases, or will this be limited? Will the locks be changed? Will he remove furniture? What about financial support? Will he be responsible for the bills? Who will pay what? Will you have to ask him for money each time it is needed (a very controlling maneuver on his part), or will a set amount be available at designated times during the month? If children are involved, how is visitation set up? When and where does he visit? All of these questions need to be answered if you are to eliminate some of the confusion regarding the separation.

Whereas living arrangements have multiple areas of concern, personal contact has only one: What is the sexual relationship between the two of you during the separation? I would guess that the majority of couples who separate continue some degree of sexual activity after the husband has left. Sometimes it is initiated by the wife, who is lonely or believes she can win him back with sex. Often it is initiated by the husband. Frequently, it is even *expected* by him: "After all, we're still married, and you are my wife." My philosophy on this issue is very clear—there is to be no sexual activity while the two of you are separated. If he chooses to return to the marriage and reconciliation is achieved, then the sexual aspect of the relationship can resume. However, short of reconciliation, any attempts to become sexually active should be strongly resisted.

Do Not Protect Him

It is not unusual for rejected wives to protect their husbands from the effects of the separation. One way of doing this is by keeping the separation a secret. I counseled one wife who successfully protected her husband's public image, at his request, for several months. This was made easier by the fact that he traveled a great deal on business. Nevertheless, through the aid of his cooperative wife, he was able to play out two roles. While he lived with a mistress during the week, he would return home on some weekends to assume his more respectable role as husband and churchman. No one suspected there was a problem.

Another way women protect their husbands is by lying about their whereabouts. One wife, although acknowledging that she and her husband were in fact separated, refused to give out his location to bill collectors. Through riotous living, he was running up large debts and not paying legitimate responsibilities such as mortgage and credit card payments. Still, she chose to take the heat from the bill collectors instead of giving them his new address.

Why do women protect these men? Why don't they tell friends about the separation? Why don't they tell family members? Why do they even keep it a secret from his parents? I frequently hear several reasons. Sometimes they fear that disclosing information about their present marital situation will only result in driving their husbands further away. Some husbands even make this threat: "If you tell anyone that I've left, you can kiss any possibility that I might come back good-bye." Others don't want to ruin his reputation in case he does decide to come back. Still others fear the possible stigma to their own image or that of their children.

Even though I can understand all of these rationales, I do not agree with them. Husbands who leave need to experience the consequences of their behavior. This is not to say that a wife goes out of her way to develop resentment in others toward her husband. But she does not protect him, either. He needs to face the reality of his decision. It will have an impact on friends. It will have an effect on relationships with children and extended family members. His church and community will have a reaction. This is reality. This is the real world. This discomfort is what he needs to experience. He is making adult decisions; allow him to be an adult and deal with the consequences.

Take Control of Self

Taking control of self involves the realization that people should not seek to control others but should strive to be responsible for their own behavior. Although you can seemingly control someone else's behavior for a period of time, this is never healthy. You are not responsible for your husband's decisions. You cannot force him to come back. But you are responsible for your behavior, and your goal is to control it. In so doing, you need to act versus react and make decisions based on healthy choices as opposed to comfortable scripts. Establish some boundaries around yourself. Determine where you stop and your husband begins. Only assume responsibility for your end of the relationship, not his.

We have a misconception regarding power in that we frequently see it as force. A man who is six feet four and three hundred pounds is considered powerful, whereas a smaller individual is not. Actually, power is better defined as "the ability to control the behavior of others." I have seen some homes where a four-year-old was the most powerful person in the family. When it comes to relationships, people have no more power over us than we allow them. One frustrated wife shared with me how throughout her marriage, her in-laws controlled her behavior. She constantly tried to please them, but she could never do enough. She was never a good-enough housekeeper; never a good-enough mother; and never a good-enough wife to their son. Finally, he left, and she feared what they would say about *her* failure. Ironically, they had no more influence over her than she gave them. Unfortunately, she had given them too much. Sometimes we do the same thing with husbands, especially when separated from them.

When you begin to take control of your life, you determine exactly what you are responsible for and assume that responsibility. But you assume no more than that, and you do not allow others to force you to do otherwise.

When you do take control of self, you also begin to do for self. By this I mean that you begin to invest some of your energies into healthy preoccupations. This may involve recreational activities, social groups, solitary hobbies, Bible studies, new friendships (as opposed to mere acquaintances), and so forth. In short, you are doing things that enrich your personal life. This is not only healthy for you as you seek an emotionally balanced life, but it also aids in your attempt to back off from your husband. Instead of pursuing him, you can invest in some healthy preoccupations. This is definitely in your best interest.

Determine Your Expectations

Finally, you need to determine exactly what you want out of the relationship, should your husband decide to come home. Or, even more importantly, what you expect to occur before you allow your husband to return. This line of reasoning implies something that is often overlooked in times of separation: Marriage is a two-vote system. This should have become painfully clear when your husband elected to leave. Your one vote in favor of the marriage did not keep the two of you together. His decision to come back is still only one vote. You also have to vote for the marriage if the two of you are going to get back together. He is not in total control, and neither are you; however, you are in control of your one vote.

My emphasis here is not to focus on power or to suggest there should be a power struggle. Rather, it's to emphasize the need for genuine reconciliation as opposed to merely settling for intactness. His decision to come back—what is it based on? Did he get lonely? Is he tired of sleeping alone? Is he coming back totally for his own self-regard? Does he care at all for you or the relationship? Or is he just looking for a place to crash for a while? Does any of this make any difference to you? It should!

You have the right to have expectations regarding both the future of your relationship and the means by which you get back together. Without genuine reconciliation, the relationship has a very dim future. Reconciliation is a legitimate expectation. What about seeing a marital therapist? Is this a legitimate expectation? The counterproductive aspects that were a part of your marriage before the separation are probably still there, and they still need to be dealt with. If he has been promiscuous, what about medical tests for venereal disease and AIDS? I know women who regretfully wish this had been one of their expectations. There are many examples of legitimate expectations. The point is, you need to determine exactly what yours are *before* you get back together—not after. There need to be as few surprises as possible once your husband finally decides to swing back into the relationship.

Letting Go of the Put-Out Husband: A Special Case

Due to the special characteristics inherent in the men who are put out of marriages, letting them go requires some additional efforts. You will recall that I described these men as highly repetitive. We are not dealing with first offenders here. Rather, these husbands demonstrated long histories of unacceptable patterns of behavior. Furthermore, they tend to be selfish and grossly unconcerned for the needs of others; the specific behavior is deviant as opposed to being merely different; and the behavior is always destructive. In short, put-out husbands tend to be emotionally unstable and have significant personality problems.

You will also recall that, of the three categories, they fare the worst emotionally with the separation. In part, this is because they are being put out as opposed to choosing to leave. But it is also related to their basic personality problem. These husbands are usually quite dependent upon their wives for emotional support. Although very controlling men, and seemingly oblivious to anyone else's needs, they need the context of the home for some sense of security. They are not generally autonomous and independent men. As a result of all these factors, their primary goal becomes getting back home and getting things right back to the way they were.

Put-out husbands are astute manipulators. They are willing to do whatever it takes in order to reach their goal of getting back home—and they know the weaknesses of their wives. Although there are many examples of manipulation, any tactic will fall into one of two categories. It will either be *coercive* or *acquiescent.* Regardless of the form, however, always remember that its goal is aimed at not changing. He wants back home, and he wants things to continue as they were.

Coercive Manipulation

There are many forms of manipulation that are coercive in nature. The major theme is the use of force. Sometimes this occurs in a violent form such as physical abuse. At other times it is in a less violent variation, yet equally abusive, as in threats and verbal intimidation. It can come in the form of withheld financial support aimed at forcing a wife to accept a husband back. I once counseled a woman who reported a long and violent marital history filled with beatings and other forms of abuse. She related that things had become so violent at one point in the marriage that she left her husband. How did he respond? He had her utilities disconnected, refused to support her financially, and harassed her at home and at work. When she lost her job because of his interference, she gave up and returned to the marriage. He had won, and the marriage continued as it had always been—abusively.

There are other ways to exercise force. Sometimes it comes in the form of peer pressure. A husband who wants to return home may seek aid from his friends or his wife's pastor. He tells them he wants to be reunited with his wife and children, to resume his role as husband and father. They then talk to her on his behalf. At other times the husband becomes helpless. "I cannot exist without you. I'm falling apart." Ultimately, he can threaten to commit suicide. This tends to unnerve even the most resolute wives. Coercion comes in many forms. What's important to remember, however, is that it is never aimed at change or reconciliation. Its only goal is the continuation of things as they were, with him in control.

Acquiescent Manipulation

Whereas coercion utilizes force, acquiescence gives the appearance of giving in. Whatever accusations are asserted by the wife, the husband fully admits. Whatever demands are made, he fully accepts. He is in total agreement with whatever she has to say.

"Just let me come home. I'll do anything you say. Whatever it takes is fine with me. I can change. I really can. Just give me another chance. I know I've made promises before, but this time it's different. Give me one more chance to prove how much I love you. You owe me that much. That's all I'm asking for. Just one more chance."

All of this may sound really good, but remember, the goal of this form of manipulation is only to get back home. Once there, the promises, the good intentions, the supposed changes are forgotten. Soon, it's business as usual.

What to Do

Because of the repetitive nature of these husbands' offenses, as well as their clear propensity to manipulate their wives in order to get what they want, letting go takes on two additional characteristics. Actually, these additional characteristics are extensions of determining your expectations. With put-out husbands, your expectations for change in your husband's behavior must be met *before* you even enter a discussion about allowing him to return. Furthermore, these behavioral changes must be demonstrated over a period of time. In essence, you are saying that his credit is no longer any good. There has to be a genuine change before any form of reconciliation can be attempted. You will no longer participate in the old game where he makes a promise that he never keeps and you let him get away with it. The rules have changed.

Some husbands see this as an attempt to control them and the relationship. Actually, this is not the case. Remember, healthy people do not try to control other people. It is, however, a wife's direct attempt to take control of her own life. She is deciding what she can live with and what she cannot. This is healthy. One thing she cannot live with is irresponsible behavior in a mate. If he wishes to continue to behave irresponsibly, that's fine. That's his choice to make, but he won't do that with her. That's her choice to make. She is not responsible for his choices, but she is for hers.

An example of this would be the case of an alcoholic husband. Rather than allowing your husband to return home because he says he will not drink anymore or that he will seek professional help for his problem, you require it on the front end, over a significant period of time.

"I intend to stay separated for at least six months. During

that time I expect you to be sober and involved in an alcohol-treatment program. If after that period of time you have maintained your sobriety and have made significant progress in your therapy program, we will discuss the possibility and means of reconciliation. If you choose not to make these changes, which is your right, I will take that as a decision not to maintain this marriage."

The same theme is expressed regardless of the form of irresponsibility—physical abuse, verbal abuse, controlling nature, promiscuity. There is nothing sacred about a particular length of time; however, it needs to be long enough to allow the opportunity for genuine change. Even with professional help, changes of this nature won't come quickly or easily.

Not New Advice

Some would say that what I proposed is not new advice. Sure, I may have clarified it more or offered some distinctive categories, but the basic suggestion to let him go has already been made. To this I would agree. Others have written the pioneering volumes that shatter the more traditional molds of "just love him back." But if working with marriages for a number of years has taught me anything, it is this: There is a great difference between knowing what to do and *doing* it. I have found that getting a rejected wife to agree to back off from her husband is a far easier task than her actually doing it. This only verifies the truth that some solutions may be simple but not easy.

The true art of therapy is not in diagnosis—the determination of the problem. This is in no way meant to lessen the importance of diagnosis; it is essential to know what the problem is in order to treat it. But once this is determined, the real challenge comes with getting people to do what they ought to do. They know what to do—they just can't do it. Unfortunately, many of the books dealing with this area of marital separation are far clearer on the "oughts" than they are on the "how-tos."

What stops you from letting him go? Why can't you do what you need to do? When it comes to letting husbands go, I find that there are a large number of factors that interfere with backing off. It is these interferences which make it difficult for a wife to do what she needs to do.

Study Questions

1. Write down your feelings and the pros and cons about the three options you face if your spouse has left:
   - Immediately divorce him.
   - Pursue him.
   - Let him go.

2. Six steps that need to be taken to let your husband go are identified in this chapter. What will be required of you to complete these steps? Be specific. (Example: under "Structure of the Separation," the chapter asks about financial support. This would be the place to write down what you expect your spouse to provide you.)

3. What is the stand you need to take?

4. In what ways should you back off?

5. How should the separation be structured? Consider finances, children, counseling, etc.

6. Do not protect him. Is this relevant to your situation? If so, how?

7. What steps do you need to take in order to take control of yourself?

8. What are your expectations?

9. If yours is the special case this chapter mentions of letting go of the put-out husband, continue detailing the steps that you need to clarify the specific problems of this situation.

Your Response

4

"I Know It's Working, But . . ."

Lisa and Tim had very different personalities. At least that's what Tim told me at our first therapy session. He was outgoing and fun loving, whereas Lisa was shy and sedate. From what I could observe in a brief period of time, Tim's assessment was accurate.

Tim was a "hip" dresser and in the entertainment field. He possessed boundless energy, and every movement of his body was expressive. His eyes danced, he talked with his hands, his facial expressions told you exactly what was going on in his head. Lisa, on the other hand, was less transparent. This is not to say that she tried to hide things, but she projected a less enthusiastic and bubbly demeanor. She was pleasant . . . relaxed . . . sedate. In her presence, I had the feeling of warmth and calm, quite a contrast to the electrifying Tim. Even her chosen career in the child-care field matched her countenance. Tim's assessment that he and Lisa had different personalities seemed quite accurate.

"We never really knew each other before we got married. I mean, we dated for quite a while, but I don't think we realized just how different we were. If we had, I don't think we would have gotten married. I know if I had it to do over again, I wouldn't do it."

Lisa's calm, pleasant demeanor could not hide the pain this statement caused her. Tim's comment, which was apparently easy for him to say, had slashed Lisa deeply.

Though I was sure this was not the first time she had heard these words, the power of his rejection was obvious. Lisa reached for a facial tissue and wiped her tears before she responded to Tim's statement.

"We are different. That's easy to see. But we've always been different. We knew this even when we were dating. It didn't seem to be a problem then, and I don't know if it's a problem now. At least, it doesn't upset me."

My tendency is to agree with Lisa on the issue of differences: They do not have to be a problem. What is important is how the difference is dealt with. Differences are to be anticipated and expected. In fact, I challenge you to show me two people who are exactly the same. When we encounter differences in a marriage, they generally necessitate adjustment.

This is not to say that differences are never problematic, because they can be, but I think we have a tendency to make too big a thing out of them. Blaming the demise of a marriage on differences is the easy out, and not necessarily accurate. This is especially the case when the differences are in the area of personality. Issues of control, selfishness, extroversion, introversion, and so forth are brought into the marriage and do require attention for blending. But if these characteristics are not *excessive* in nature, two fairly mature and emotionally healthy individuals ought to be able to resolve them.

I actually find far more significant difficulties when the differences between mates are in the areas of values or expectations. When one is religious and the other is not, when one wants companionship and the other wants convenience, the differences can be major, and resolving them is often a difficult task.

The differences in personality that Tim described did not strike me as the kind of problem that would destroy a marriage. Lisa and Tim's marriage may have been on its last leg, but if it was, it wasn't because they differed in their expressiveness.

"Why are you here? What do you want to see changed? What do you want to happen as a result of being in therapy?" I try to ask questions of this nature fairly early in the first session because the answers provide me with a great deal of information. Usually there is reference made to complaints about the past, dissatisfactions with the present, and goals for the future. All of this is essential data as I plan a strategy for helping the couple resolve their marital difficulty. Oftentimes, however, I gain a further insight into their motivation for therapy or, for lack of a better choice of words, their readiness to work on the marriage. The responses Lisa and Tim gave to this line of questioning provided a strong clue regarding their readiness for marital therapy. "I just want Tim to love me. I want him to care. I want to be able to touch him without him cringing. He is so distant."

With this statement, Lisa once again began to cry. As she continued, she described, and Tim confirmed, a dismal five-year marital relationship. It seemed that the early interference of Lisa's family in the life of the newly married couple prompted resentment in Tim. He felt that Lisa should be more supportive of his position, but he had never dealt directly with her about it. Instead, he invested more energy in his work and less in his marriage. In short, he avoided his problem with Lisa and began the long and gradual process of emotional distancing.

The tendency to avoid conflict, which came so easily to Tim, came just as naturally to Lisa. She sensed his drifting away, but she was confused because she didn't know the reason for Tim's withdrawal or how to stop it. Regretfully, Lisa just continued to suffer in silence as Tim went on with his life.

Probably the most obviously noticeable indication that something was wrong was in their sex life, which had changed tremendously. During the last three years, the frequency of their sexual activity could be measured in intervals of years as opposed to days, weeks, or even months. It is quite common for the sexual relationship of a couple to provide a glimpse into the emotional well-being of a marriage.

Still, even with this dramatic change, nothing was said. They never discussed the sexual deficiencies of their marriage or the widening emotional gulf that had grown between them. Yet even though the emotional distance was not discussed, it remained a very present concern. At least it remained a concern for Lisa, and her statement, "I just want Tim to love me," provided a wealth of information.

Tim's response was equally enlightening but far less encouraging. "I don't know what I want. If you had asked me that question three weeks ago, I would have said I want a separation. In fact, when I approached Lisa about a separation, she suggested we see a counselor. But now . . . I just don't know. I don't know if I could stand to be away from my children. If it wasn't for that, I'd probably already be gone. I just don't know what I want."

Tim reached over and patted Lisa on the arm in an effort to console her. It was obvious that what he had just stated was not easy for him to say. He was not a cold and callous man, only a pushed-out man. "I don't want to hurt you, Lisa. But we need to get it all out here." She managed to smile back at him. But Lisa's appreciation for Tim's caring enough to console her hardly equaled her disappointment in his verbal rejection.

What I learned from their responses was that Lisa wanted to work on the marriage, while Tim did not. True, Tim didn't say that—he only said he was not sure what he did want. It's been my experience as a therapist that when it comes to determining just how much effort will be exerted toward working on a marriage, "I don't know" doesn't count for much. In fact, it's usually a *no* in disguise. So as I looked at this couple, it was fairly clear to me that Lisa was willing to work toward restoring the relationship but Tim was not. And from a marriage therapist's perspective, this is a fairly low-percentage shot.

When faced with the dilemma of one mate voting for the marriage and the other voting against, the possibility of a separation looms greater as an option than it does when both mates are interested in keeping the marriage together. After talking about what would be required if we pursued traditional marital therapy, I broached the option of a trial separation. Neither Lisa nor Tim wanted to pursue this line of thought. Although less resistant to the idea than Lisa, even Tim chose to try traditional marital therapy first, so another appointment was set, with the stipulation that some special tests were to be completed before our next session.

What followed was six weeks of cancellations. Lisa would set an appointment, only to call and cancel it due to a last-minute schedule conflict for Tim. Furthermore, whereas Lisa had quickly completed the assigned testing, Tim had failed to complete his. It began to appear as though a second appointment would not take place. Finally, Lisa called and talked to me directly about her problem.

"I keep working out appointment times around Tim's schedule, but he keeps coming up with last-minute conflicts. I know he hasn't completed the tests, either. I don't know what else to do. I think he's stalling, but he denies that. All I know is that I'm getting frustrated with what's happening. Things between Tim and me are getting worse. What should I do?"

Lisa's voice was no longer demure; six weeks of foot-dragging had taken its toll. She seemed ready to take more control of her situation. I suggested that Lisa set an appointment and then inform Tim of her intention to keep it, regardless of whether he did or not. She didn't need to threaten him, only take a stand, make a statement, and follow through. Lisa said she would do as I suggested. When Tim completed his testing the day before the scheduled appointment, I felt reasonably certain that Lisa had spoken with him and he would be accompanying her to the session. I was correct.

The atmosphere of the second session was quite a bit different from the first. As I had suspected, six weeks of noncommitted foot-dragging on the part of Tim had added frustration to Lisa's already present feelings of hurt. This new dimension seemed to make her angry enough to take some action. Her demeanor had changed. She was not vindictive, but her pleasantness had been replaced with decisiveness. She was ready for things to change.

Tim, on the other hand, was a little more subdued. He was far from totally quiet, but it was clear that his previous happy-go-lucky attitude had diminished. He was more anxious. He would sigh deeply, as if to suggest that he was weighted down with trying to make a decision. Indeed, he was caught in the throes of a dilemma: to leave or not to leave. What should he do? Some of his pressure undoubtedly came from the fact that he was no longer totally in the driver's seat. Lisa was rejecting her previous role of passive responder, and with this change came increased tension for Tim.

I began the session by inquiring about the status of the relationship. "It's been six weeks since we last got together. What's happened between the two of you? Anything?"

Tim spoke first. He began by stating that things were just as they had been. He still didn't know what he wanted to do. He wished that he did, but he just wasn't sure. He seemed to be resigning himself to an existence of indecision.

Lisa agreed that things were no different, but the fact that there had been no change in Tim had prompted a change in Lisa. Tim's indecision was taking its toll, and she was ready to do something. Anything was better than sitting and waiting.

I discussed the testing material that both Tim and Lisa had completed. It confirmed what they had reported and I had observed: Lisa was interested in the marriage and Tim was not. So what should they do?

"What's keeping the two of you together?" There was no response. Once again, I brought up the option of a therapeutic separation. My goal was not to ease Tim and Lisa into a divorce. To the contrary, I wanted them to rebuild their marriage, but they were not ready to do that, and I thought a separation might help. Unlike our first session, both now believed this would be a good thing to do. Tim was a little more hesitant than Lisa, but Lisa's willingness to try anything to break their marital impasse made it an easier decision for Tim. The remainder of the session was spent defining the conditions of the separation and establishing what my role would be for each of them.

And what would be my role? Therapeutically, I would have consistent contact with Lisa. After all, she was the rejectee and would be in the worse pain. Lisa and I needed to deal with those things that would interfere with her letting Tim go, as well as determine under what conditions he could return.

My contact with Tim would be more sporadic. He was the rejector. As a pushed-out husband, he would experience some predictable anxiety, but he could be expected to have less emotional difficulty than Lisa. With less emotional disturbance, he would have more difficulty recognizing his need for counsel. Incidentally, my goal in working with husbands during this phase of treatment is not to give aid and comfort. Rather, I focus on their own shortcomings and contributions to the marital deterioration. I want them to recognize their role in the failure of the relationship and assume some responsibility for rebuilding it.

When the terms of the therapeutic separation were understood by both Tim and Lisa, they left my office to begin a new phase of their relationship. Although neither was following the course of action they had initially envisioned when they first sought marital therapy, at least some movement was finally being made.

What followed was several weeks of difficult adjustments. I met with Lisa on a regular basis, attempting to provide emotional support and direction. It is one thing to talk about a separation and quite another to actually live one. Gradually, however, Lisa began to gain greater and greater control of her situation. It was difficult to balance the functional demands of a job, children, and household activities, but Lisa began to manage. Through increased contact with girlfriends, she began to strengthen her support network, and with time, she began to do some things for herself.

It is not unusual for wives in marriages like Lisa's to neglect themselves. Although it is possible to become too self-centered, it is also possible to become so involved with the needs of others that your own needs go unserviced. Much like our body's need for a balanced diet, our emotional selves also need a balanced diet. When it comes to interests and activities, couples fare best when they are involved in "his, hers, and theirs." By this I mean that he needs to have his activities, she needs to have hers, and they need to have their corporate interests and activities. I took this opportunity to encourage Lisa to get more into herself and pursue some of her own personal interests. She took me up on my advice and joined a spa. This particular choice offered the added advantage of physical exercise.

By gaining greater control of her situation and doing some things for herself, the task of giving Tim some space was made much easier. Lisa found herself fairly calm. She had her anxious moments, but for the most part she felt good about where things were in the relationship. As the weeks went by, Lisa's ability to calmly give Tim some rope began to have an effect. Slowly, Tim began to demonstrate a renewed interest in both Lisa and the marriage. The first indication was an increase in the quantity of contact: Tim began to call and visit more frequently. This was followed by an improvement in the quality of contact. Tim began to be more pleasant and seemed to demonstrate a genuine interest in Lisa as a person.

I saw all of this as positive. After all, wasn't this our goal? Didn't we want to allow Tim some space in the hope that he would resolve his frustration and be motivated to return to Lisa and invest in the relationship? Even though things do not always work out this way, our goal is always true reconciliation. So with things going in a positive direction, you can imagine my concern when Lisa arrived for a therapy session in an obvious state of perplexity.

I began the session by asking Lisa how things were going with Tim.

"I guess they couldn't be going better. Tim's wanting to spend more time with me. He's suggested we go out on some dates. Can you imagine that? Married for five years and now we're going to start dating. There's got to be a little humor in that."

I then asked Lisa what she thought about Tim's suggestion.

"I like the idea. I haven't seen Tim this interested in me since before we got married. I've made it a point to be direct and emotionally honest with him instead of sitting on my feelings. He seems to be doing the same. When we talk on the phone, he tells me that he really cares about me. And now he speaks in terms of *when* we get back together instead of *if* we get back together. This is what I have wanted to happen."

I figured it was time to see what was perplexing Lisa. "If things are going so well," I asked, "why do you appear so troubled?"

Lisa sat quietly in her chair for a few moments. Her silence did not appear to be due to shock from my question. Rather, it seemed that she was searching for the words that would truly express her thoughts. Finally she responded, "I know that what I'm doing is working. Tim and I both are really making some changes. For the first time in many years, it looks as though our relationship may have a chance. But I can't help feeling that what I'm doing is not what I'm *supposed* to be doing."

There it was. There was the problem, the perplexity, the thing that was obviously troubling Lisa. Although letting Tim go was working, it was not what Lisa thought she was supposed to be doing. It didn't feel right, and this troubled her.

With this statement, Lisa's perplexity was no longer a mystery. Once she said, "It's not what I'm supposed to be doing," the situation was clarified. Once I began to understand what was happening, it was no longer surprising to me that the visible success of things getting better did little to relieve her feeling of discomfort.

Inside Lisa's mind, a debate was raging. On the one hand, there was a voice advising her to let Tim go: *Back off and give Tim some space.* On the other hand, there was a voice arguing against this philosophy: *There is a right way and a wrong way, and this is wrong.* What was Lisa to do? How could she end the struggle? What was the right thing to do?

I have deliberately taken the liberty of describing Lisa's situation in such detail because of the importance of her remarks. "It's not what I'm supposed to be doing" represents an argument against the let-him-go philosophy, and arguments of this nature can be very powerful.

Arguments against the let-him-go philosophy are powerful interferences because they attack the woman's belief system. When you influence what people believe, you also influence how they behave. It is far easier to deal with the problems associated with letting a husband go when you believe it is the correct thing to do. In Lisa's case, even though what she was doing was working, unless she resolved the debate in her mind, she wouldn't be able to continue this behavior. Instead, she would once again pursue him in ways that were not only self-defeating, but defeating for the relationship as well.

Arguments against the let-him-go philosophy come in different forms. In my years as a marital therapist, I have encountered four such arguments with some degree of frequency. Each is powerful as a potential influencer of behavior.

"It Doesn't Seem Christian"

This particular argument is what troubled Lisa and caused her to wonder whether she was doing the right thing. As a Christian wife, was she supposed to be letting Tim go, or was she supposed to be "loving him back"?

Lisa did not arrive at this perplexing point all on her own. She had lots of help. First of all, she had many years of culture that contributed to this argument. Raised in the church, Lisa found that her deeply ingrained value system resisted the type of philosophy that would let a husband go. She had been taught that true Christian love was giving, and the appropriate duty of a wife was to not make waves. She was responsible for making the marriage work. If she only held on a little longer and loved him a little harder, God would honor her diligence by saving her marriage.

In addition to being culturally predisposed to a different value system, Lisa also had some present-tense Christian friends who challenged the let-him-go philosophy. They argued that this approach was not Christian. The Christian thing to do in a marriage like hers was to love Tim back. Through the combined efforts of culture and friends, Lisa was sensing a great deal of pressure to abandon her present course of action for a more "appropriate" form of behavior—a course of action that was "Christian."

I believe that there are some major tenets of faith upon which we conservative evangelicals rest our beliefs. These are the essentials that most denominations hold in common. They are clear and concise, and leave little room for dispute. Excluding these major issues, there are many other issues which, because of their lesser degree of importance or their lack of clarity, offer us potential for disagreement.

Where these lesser issues are concerned, I personally have great difficulty with any position that purports to be *the* Christian position, suggesting that any other viewpoint, by the very fact that it is different, is therefore "less" Christian, if not entirely "non" Christian. It is difficult to gain clear direction on many of these lesser issues. If this were not the case, we would have fewer denominations, since it is differences of interpretation over these minor issues that divide us into different denominational groupings.

Differences over minor issues do not have to be divisive. It would be great if we all agreed on everything, but we know this is not reality. There is too little clarity in Scripture for this to happen. For example, the same Paul who said, "If eating meat offends my brother, then I won't eat meat" *(see* 1 Corinthians 8:13) also said, "Why let people dictate to you" (Colossians 2:20). The fact that he was once again dealing with the issue of eating meat is shown in verse 16: "Allow no one therefore to take you to task about what you eat. . . ."

In and of themselves, both of these are clear statements of Paul's position. Our difficulty comes with trying to reconcile what has the appearance of being contradictory stands. I can personally make sense out of what Paul was saying, but my personal interpretation may not be the understanding you derive. Which of us would be correct? Who would be right and who would be wrong?

Would it really make any significant difference? Does it really matter? I think not. For it was also Paul who, once again addressing these "lesser issues" (including that of eating meat), had this to say: ". . . On such a point everyone should have reached conviction in his own mind" (Romans 14:5).

In essence, there are many lesser issues that we have to resolve for ourselves, and the fact that we differ in how we resolve them is only of minor significance. As long as we are both seeking the Lord's leadership in our lives and our decisions have a biblical basis, we are far better off exercising tolerance toward one another than we are in proclaiming to have the one and only Christian solution.

I believe that what I am suggesting in this book is biblically based and Christian. However, I do not want to imply that this is the only approach to this problem. I do believe it is the best, but regardless of my personal preference for the let-him-go philosophy, I don't want to be guilty of claiming it is *the* Christian position. There are other views that could claim to have a biblical basis, and each one of you is responsible for reaching "conviction in his own mind."

When we look to Scripture for guidance, we find that it instructs us both directly and indirectly. We receive direct instruction when we are told specifically what to do. These are the "thou shalts" and "thou shalt nots." Indirect instruction, on the other hand, comes in the form of examples and demonstrations. Rather than being told what to do, we learn through observing the lives of others.

In support of the argument that letting him go is consistent with a Christian philosophy, I want to cite two scriptural passages, both of the latter category of instruction. They are Scriptures of example whereby, through observation, we learn how to behave. With Jesus and Paul providing us the examples for emulation, we cannot stray too far.

The first example of letting him go is Jesus' description of the prodigal son (Luke 15:11–32). We are all familiar with the story. The son wanted his inheritance. He was tired of the dull existence offered by life on a farm. He found it lifeless and frustrating. He yearned for excitement. The riotous life-style of a "distant country" beckoned him to come out, so he sought what was due him from his father and planned to leave.

What did the father do? How did he react? Did he refuse his son's request? "No! You cannot have your money. I forbid you to leave!" Did the father feverishly cling to his son? "Quick! All you servants. Come here and restrain my son. He wants to leave, and I do not want him to go." Or, did he kick the errant son out of his house? "Get out and never come back. I regret the day you were born. I hope you starve to death." The story is a little sketchy about the son's departure, but it appears that the father, who loved his son, simply honored the request for his inheritance and then let him go.

Let's also consider an incident recorded by Paul in his first letter to Timothy. Paul was giving Timothy a challenge to fight gallantly and to do so "armed with faith and a good conscience." But after offering these words of inspiration, Paul diverged briefly to reflect on some of the brethren who had been less than responsible in their faith.

"So fight gallantly, armed with faith and a good conscience. It was through spurning conscience that certain persons made shipwreck of their faith, among them Hymenaeus and Alexander, whom I consigned to Satan, in the hope that through this discipline they might learn not to be blasphemous" (1 Timothy 1:19, 20).

So while Timothy was fighting the good fight, some of the other Christian brethren were erring, apparently in great measure, making no effort to change their behavior. Had they made such an effort, they would have obviously been forgiven, reconciliation would have taken place, and there would have been no further need for action on Paul's part. But since Paul had to deal with them in a disciplinary manner, we know that these men were continuing in their irresponsibility.

What do these two passages have to do with husbands leaving their wives? Both of these are examples of letting him go. One is an example of a *passive* letting him go; the other is an example of a more *active* form. But both represent the same philosophy, and both strive for the same goal.

In the case of the prodigal son, we are witnessing the more passive form of letting him go. This is most applicable to those instances where husbands are either pulled or pushed out of their marriages. Just as the father in this story realized he could not restrain his son, wives faced with similar circumstances need to let their husbands go.

Whereas the story of the prodigal son illustrates the passive form of letting him go, Paul's disciplinary action regarding the continued irresponsible behavior of the brethren illustrates the active form of the philosophy. In regard to husbands who leave wives, these would be in the put-out category. Because of flagrant, repetitive, unremorseful, and unchanged irresponsible behavior, Paul took definite action, just as wives do when they put out irresponsible husbands.

Even though there are differences in how these two forms of the let-him-go philosophy are acted out, what is emphatically similar is their goal. Neither one is punitive in nature. Neither one has as its primary goal the idea of making the errant pay for his behavior. True, there are always consequences to what we choose to do. But in both of these cases, whether it be the response of the father or the response of Paul, both hoped that their particular form of letting him go would result in reconciliation.

True reconciliation requires the genuine effort of both

parties, which we see in the illustration of the prodigal son. As the story proceeded, the son "came to his senses" and returned remorsefully to his father. The father's letting him go allowed for true reconciliation. We don't know the result of Paul's actions; however, there is no mistaking his intent. Paul stated that he hoped "they might learn not to be blasphemous" (v. 20).

It's noteworthy that Paul referred to his act of letting them go as discipline. That's probably what it is, and as we read in Hebrews 12:10 and 11, God's discipline is always goal directed: "They disciplined us for this short life according to their lights; but he does so for our true welfare, so that we may share his holiness. Discipline, no doubt, is never pleasant; at the time it seems painful, but in the end it yields for those who have been trained by it the peaceful harvest of an honest life."

Letting him go, whether in its passive or active form, is done in the hope and anticipation that the erring husband will "come to his senses" and return, genuinely seeking reconciliation. I believe letting him go is an act of love. Granted, it's a difficult act to perform, but if it is an act of love, then it is truly an attempt at "loving him back."

"But We Ought to Be Working on the Relationship"

This argument seems to make sense. Ideally, estranged mates "ought" to be working on their relationship instead of living apart. They ought to be determining what they need from each other and what they are willing to give; what their personal contribution to the marital failure has been, and what they should do to correct it; what they need to forgive and be forgiven. But alas, this is not always what occurs.

Our problem rests with the vast gulf that often exists between the ideal and reality. Even though working on the relationship is the ideal, in reality, mates frequently fail to do what they should. Years of experience have taught me to deal with what is real, not with what is ideal.

What is real when a husband leaves his wife is that he is questioning his commitment to the marriage. What is real is that he is being controlled by his emotions and not by his intellect. And what is also very real is that he does not want to work on the relationship. At least, he does not want to work on it at this particular point in time. All of this is reality, and it is reality that we have to deal with, not the ideal.

A frantic wife may cling to the notion that she and her husband ought to be working on the relationship. If she does, this rationale will cause her to resist the let-him-go philosophy. She will either back off in an anxious and halfhearted manner, or she will resist the philosophy altogether and continue to pursue him. Either way, she is living in a world of fantasy. Rather than dealing with reality, she is choosing to deal with the ideal, and this behavior leads only to futility.

Reality tells us that a husband and wife are only ready to work on their marital relationship when they are *both* ready. In times of separation, unless the husband is genuinely swinging back into the marriage, there is only one person ready to work on the relationship—the wife. With this state of affairs, *they* are not ready. Any serious work on a relationship is always preceded by genuine reconciliation.

Yes, the couple should be working on their relationship, but this argument only serves as an interference to productive behavior in a marital separation. First things first. You have to let the husband go in the hope that he will come to his senses and present the opportunity for truly working on the relationship.

"But I Was at Fault, Too"

I met with Tom and Brenda for three sessions before Tom decided on a separation. Actually, they were informally separated before coming to therapy. Tom lived in one bedroom while Brenda lived in another. It was the tension of that arrangement that brought them to my office in the first place.

Tom wanted a separation from the beginning but felt therapy was the responsible thing to do. Talking about what would have to happen for their marriage to work only increased Tom's anxiety. As a classic pushed-out husband, the only solution he saw was getting out. He needed some space, and he needed it now.

Brenda was admittedly a pushy woman. From the moment they first met, she had seen real potential in Tom. With a little help, Brenda believed he could really amount to something, so she took him on as a project.

> Tom and I came from two very different backgrounds. He's the proverbial poor boy who makes good, whereas my family always had money. What attracted me to Tom was his strong desire to achieve and his religious commitment. I felt that with a little polishing up, he could be very successful.
>
> I realize now that I probably tried to do too much. I should have let Tom be Tom. But I was only trying to help him out. Everything I did was for his good. But I don't have to do that anymore.

Tom described Brenda more as a doting mother than a wife. Although he tried to resist her tendencies to control him earlier in the marriage, that had generally led to an argument. He gradually learned to avoid the conflict by staying away from home and passively (but sullenly) giving in to all of Brenda's suggestions.

Brenda selects and purchases all of my clothes. She doesn't think my taste in clothing is appropriate for a person of my status. On most days she even lays out what I am supposed to wear. Apparently I don't know how to talk, either. She is constantly correcting my speech. And as far as manners go, I guess I'm the world's worst.

You know, I can only take so much. I feel like I can't even breathe at home. I don't know why she even married me in the first place. We are so different.

I need to be me, and I don't think Brenda can let that happen. I can never be what she wants me to be, and she will never stop trying to "correct" me. She can't change.

That was the way things were when Tom decided to leave Brenda. He said he only wanted a separation, but he could not guarantee that he would come back to the marriage. All Tom knew at the time was that he needed some space and some time to think.

I continued to see Brenda on a regular basis and encouraged her to allow Tom to have the space he desired. This was a difficult thing for Brenda to do. Remember, she was pushy. What served to complicate the situation further, however, was Brenda's realization that she had been guilty of "crossing Tom's boundaries" and the belief that she had changed. "Tom is right. I was wrong for trying to change him as I did. I should have let him be himself. I realize that now, and I believe I am a different person. Somehow I've got to prove that to Tom. He has to see that I have changed. I can't show him if he's living in one place and I'm living in another. I've got to get him back."

I will agree that Brenda had crossed Tom's boundaries during most of their marriage. She was correct in assuming some responsibility for the deterioration of her marriage, but that's true in most marriages. I see few relationships where one mate wears a black hat and one wears a white hat. Usually both hats are a little gray in color, and there is opportunity for both mates to feel somewhat guilty.

But this doesn't change the facts. The bottom line was that Tom was not ready to deal with the relationship. Until he was, Brenda would not have the opportunity to prove anything.

She couldn't allow her guilt to act as a rationale for pursuing Tom. Her being wrong didn't change the fact that Tom wasn't ready to deal with the marriage. Nor did it change our approach. She needed to continue to let him go.

Brenda could inform Tom that she had made some headway regarding her need to correct him and that she believed she had changed. She could also reaffirm her commitment to the marriage and her desire to demonstrate that she is a different person. But after that declaration, she needed to back off. To pursue any more would only demonstrate the pushy attitude she claimed to have changed.

Brenda might have had something to prove to Tom, but she had to let him go in order to get the chance to prove it. Being at fault cannot become a rationale for pursuing.

"It Seems I'm Giving Up on the Marriage"

Letting a husband go is far from giving up on a marriage, and it is definitely not intended to encourage divorce. Some people mistakenly believe that if you are doing anything other than trying to convince a husband to stay in a marriage, you're encouraging him to pursue a divorce. I don't share this belief.

Letting a husband go is not giving up on the marriage. Rather, it's an effort to save it. Letting him go is a far more constructive attempt at saving a marriage than any other alternative. It's definitely superior to either reacting in the same fashion as the departing husband or pursuing him.

The goal of letting him go is not divorce, but reconciliation. True, divorce may result, but this is possible regardless of what the wife does. Those who pursue this approach of dealing with a departing husband do so because of the potential for saving the marriage, not for ending it.

"I know it's working, but it's not what I'm supposed to be doing." The real problem with these arguments against the let-him-go philosophy is that they are subtle interferences. They prevent you from doing what you need to do. At a time when action is needed, you react instead. At a time when control of self is necessary, you give control to your departing husband. At a time when a constructive plan is essential, you are paralyzed. Obsessed with doing the "right" thing and fearful that you may do something that will cause him never to return, you vacillate between trying to win him back and doing nothing at all. And the arguments we just discussed steadily add fuel to your confusion.

Study Questions

1. In the course of your separation you may be troubled and think your actions are not what you are supposed to be doing. Take some time and write out your recurring doubts and why (or why not) you think they are appropriate thoughts.

2. In this chapter, several recurring, troublesome thoughts are mentioned. Have the following thoughts affected you? If so, how?
   - We ought to be working on the relationship.
   - I was at fault, too.
   - It seems I'm giving up on the marriage.

Your Response

_____

_____

_____

_____

_____

_____

_____

_____

_____

_____

_____

Part Two

INTERFERENCES

5

Troublesome
Emotions

When I first met with Cindy, she and Jimmy were already separated. In fact, it was the sixth separation in their short two and one-half years of marriage. The scenario for all six separations had been the same. Cindy would get upset with Jimmy's neglect of her and her son. Jimmy would accuse Cindy of trying to control his life. "If I want to spend time with my friends, I'll do it." He would then storm out of the house and speed away in his truck. Upon arriving at his parents' house, Jimmy would call and inform Cindy that he was not coming home. He would tell her that he felt trapped there. He had to have his freedom. Cindy would then apologize for her behavior and plead with him to return. Jimmy would refuse. After two or three days, however, he would stop by the house unannounced, claim he wanted to see his son, end up sleeping with Cindy, and then move back in with her the next day.

This time, however, things were different. First, Jimmy was staying away longer than usual. It had already been over a week, and he had not yet returned. Second, Cindy wanted the cycle to stop. Two and one-half years of waiting for things to get better had taken their toll on both her and the relationship. Having recently made a decision to go back to work, Cindy would soon be in a position to support herself. If the past two and one-half years were an example of what she could expect for the rest of her married life, then maybe she needed to rethink her commitment. The third factor that made this separation different was that Cindy sought counseling. On all the other occasions she simply sought consolation and advice from her friends as she waited for Jimmy to return. This time Cindy realized the need for change. She was desperate—so desperate that she went to a professional.

I began to work with Cindy with a first-things-first, let-him-go philosophy. We couldn't deal with the marriage until we dealt with the separation, and in order to deal with the separation, Cindy had to let Jimmy go. The power Jimmy exerted in their relationship was tremendous, so Cindy had to take responsibility for herself if the marriage were to have a chance of surviving. We began by defining the old, non-productive patterns that seemed to control their interaction. By doing so, we also identified Cindy's role and contribution to this cycle, which would have to change. We could easily anticipate Jimmy's next move: He would swing back into the marriage without true reconciliation. He would desire intactness, but he would not want to deal with the past. If Jimmy had his way, there would be no discussion of the incident that prompted him to leave this time. Neither would he want to talk about the real root issue in their relationship— their expectations for the marriage and their (un)willingness to be both "givers" and "receivers." This pattern of non-resolution and avoidance had to cease, but to stop it, Cindy had to do something different.

True to form, when I next saw Cindy she reported that Jimmy had unexpectedly stopped by to see his son. They then slept together, and Jimmy spent the night. When he got up the next morning to go to work, Cindy told him that she loved him but was concerned about what was happening in their marriage. She asked if he would see a counselor with her. Jimmy became upset and stormed out once again, claiming he would not be back. Cindy was crushed; she felt used and defeated.

I sat quietly for a few moments and then I asked her, "Where are the surprises?" Cindy seemed a little shocked by my question, but I pointed out that they'd just had another reenactment of the old pattern. She hadn't changed a thing, so why should she expect anything different from Jimmy?

As you can probably guess, my previous advice to Cindy had been that she take control of her part of the relationship. This would have involved her structuring the separation. In my opinion, when mates are separated, they should not sleep together or spend the night together. These things are done after mates are reconciled. Obviously, this is not what Cindy did. We knew Jimmy's next move; we had dealt with what an appropriate response to it would be in our first session, yet Cindy was unable to carry it out. Why?

That's the question I asked Cindy, although I already knew the answer, because I had heard it frequently enough from other wives in similar situations. But it was an answer that she needed to give and an issue we needed to resolve. "It's hard to say no to Jimmy. I really love him. Without him I feel so alone and empty. I just need him so much. I wish that I didn't want to be with him. Then it would be easy. But I do—and that makes it hard."

What Cindy's statement expressed and her behavior demonstrated was the result of troublesome emotions. In this particular case, she was overwhelmed by her own aloneness. "I wish I didn't want to be with him. Then it would be easy. But I do—and that makes it hard." Cindy's own emotional neediness prompted her to do things that were not in her best interest or the best interest of the relationship. Rather than structuring the separation and changing the destructive avoidance cycle that controlled her marriage, Cindy's extreme need to be loved by Jimmy compelled her to respond to his wishes. In short, she reacted instead of acting.

When a wife is overcome by her own emotional neediness, her desire to be close to her husband interferes with her doing what needs to be done. She tries to make contact with him. She shows up at his job, she calls him on the phone, she gives in to his requests. "Anything—just let me be close. The pain of being alone is unbearable." Ironically, acting in this manner is never satisfying and only results in making the wife more miserable than she already is.

"I feel so alone. It's worse at night. I think that if I could just talk with him, things would be better. So I call him. We talk for a while, but then we hang up and I always feel worse. I am always so frustrated after I call."

It is not difficult to understand why things are worse. She calls because of a need to be emotionally close—a need he cannot meet. In calling, she realizes that, which only increases her frustration and pain.

Feeling emotionally needy—alone, lonely, and empty—is one example of troublesome emotions. There is another. Anger frequently interferes with a wife doing what she needs to do when her husband has left her. This troublesome emotion is poignantly illustrated by a conversation I had with one of my clients.

"I feel like I could kill him. How could he do this to me? And how could he treat his own daughter like this? Emily is crushed. She cries every night at bedtime and asks, 'When is Daddy coming home?' I don't know what to say. It hurts me to see what he's doing to her.

"I am so angry that I can't be civil to him. Telephone calls turn into screaming matches, and when he comes by, we almost come to blows. It's terrible. I lose all control. I'm beginning to really hate him."

Women who are overcome with anger behave inappropriately. They find themselves pursuing their departed husband, but instead of clinging to him and pleading for his return, their overinvolvement is in the form of "ventilation." They call him on the telephone to tell him off. They go to his apartment to set him straight. They call his boss to fix his wagon. They are mad, and they want him to pay.

I remember one wife who had been totally devastated by her husband's departure. We worked on her letting him go, but it was very difficult because she was consumed with her neediness. All of a sudden, she came to one session extremely angry. "I want a divorce!" I hear statements like this frequently enough to know when they are genuine and when they are not. This particular wife was not really ready for divorce. She was merely overwhelmed with her anger. I asked her why she was ready for a divorce now, whereas only a week earlier it required all her resources not to pursue him.

"I'm tired of hurting. I don't want to feel this way any longer. I'm tempted to go out and sleep with another man just to get even. If he can do it, why can't I? I'll show him."

This was anger talking. She was still very much emotionally attached to her husband and only wanted to strike out and make him hurt as much as she hurt. By the following week, her anger had subsided and she realized the foolishness of her statement. Some women fail to realize this until they have also acted foolishly.

Frequently a wife will experience both these emotions, sometimes simultaneously. She will fluctuate from being overwhelmed by emotional neediness to being consumed with anger. At other times, there is a clearer movement from one phase to the other. She is first needy. But after weeks of pleading, she becomes angry. Actually, I would rather have a wife mad than sad. It seems to make therapy much more productive. Whether it's a case of neediness or anger, however, these emotional reactions are normal, not the feelings of a deranged or inept woman. They are the natural and predictable emotions encountered with this kind of loss.

The emotional bonding that takes place between mates is similar to that which occurs between parent and child. We become emotionally attached to each other, investing ourselves in another human being. We commit, we trust, we allow ourselves to be vulnerable. We do this because of our need to be close and intimate with another person and because of our personal attraction to him. Usually, this offers us the potential for a great deal of pleasure, because there is satisfaction in closeness. On a more pessimistic note, however, this closeness also carries the potential for agony. When emotional attachments are severed or interrupted, as they are in times of marital separation, we experience pain. It's really a paradox. We have to invest if we are to experience the *gains* of closeness. However, it's because of this investment that we are susceptible to the *pains* of separation.

Troublesome emotions—whether in the form of neediness or anger, our true difficulty doesn't rest with their mere occurrence. They are natural, normal reactions of wives who have been abandoned by their husbands. Our problem rests with how much control these predictable emotions have over our actions. How much will neediness be allowed to dictate behavior? How much will anger be allowed to interfere with a wife doing what she needs to do? Control is the real issue. Will it be a wife's emotional system (E) or her intellectual system (I) that directs her? Viewing it as a mathematical equation, will she function emotionally (and irrationally) with the $^E/_I$, or will she be goal directed and operate with the $^I/_E$? This is the real question.

A Common Fear

In attempting to enable wives to take control of their troublesome emotions, I have found a common fear. Here are three variations of that fear. Each wife stated it differently, but the same theme is present in each situation.

Suzanne: "I want to be all right—to not hurt—but not if it means I'm over him. It's as if I'm afraid of getting better because if I do, it will be over."

Marti: "If getting better means I stop caring for him, then I don't want to get better."

Betty: "If I get better then I won't want him, and that's scary."

This fear of no longer caring nearly paralyzes these wives. Think of the power of the emotions represented in these statements. They are so attached to their husbands that they would rather go on in severe pain than stop caring for these men!

I'm not trying to get wives to stop caring for their husbands. This can happen, and usually does, if he continues to swing out of the marriage for a long-enough period of time. Gradually, a rejected wife begins to disengage emotionally or unhook from the marriage. But this noncaring is not my goal. My aim is to reduce the control their caring has over their behavior. You can continue to care—just change what you *do*.

Taking Control of Troublesome Emotions

Troublesome emotions of neediness and anger are normal for those who are abandoned. They are expected, and should be accepted. You're not crazy if you feel them, and their elimination is not our goal. Our objective is to gain greater control of them, because they prompt nonproductive behavior. We cannot eliminate these feelings, but we can reduce the control they have on your behavior. During my years of counseling, I have found four activities to be helpful in taking control of troublesome emotions. Which of these are you presently doing?

Focus on Yourself

When a wife becomes overwhelmed by her aloneness, she becomes obsessed with her need for her husband. All she can envision is him. She needs him to "fill her up," to return and remove the void that engulfs her. This is what motivates her to pursue him. In order to counteract this excessive dependency upon her husband, I encourage her to assume responsibility for meeting some of her own needs.

Focus on yourself. Rather than waiting for your husband to come and make you feel good, what are some things that you can do for yourself? What do you like to do? What have you wanted to do but never seemed to have time to fit in? Treat yourself nice! Do some things for yourself.

Moving from a passive, waiting posture to one of assuming responsibility for yourself is a productive step. For some women, it's a totally new experience. Even in the days when the marriage was good, they never took responsibility for their own needs. They never assessed what they liked or didn't like. They never did anything for themselves. Instead, they always focused on doing for others and assumed that their needs would also be met. It didn't work well in the marriage, and it certainly doesn't work during a separation. Invest in yourself.

Be Involved in Healthy Preoccupations

Clearly related to focusing on yourself is involving yourself with healthy preoccupations. Some of these activities will come as a result of your previous self-appraisal of your needs and interests—your doing for yourself. Others will arise because of convenience and necessity. Examples of healthy preoccupations are work, hobbies, recreational activities, physical exercise, devotional times, and organized Bible studies.

When you involve yourself in healthy preoccupations, you emotionally balance your life. Just as your physical body requires a balanced diet in order to maintain physical health, your emotional self has a similar need. It, too, must have balance to be healthy. To become obsessed with one aspect of your existence to the exclusion of all others—a tendency during a separation—is emotionally unhealthy. It only fosters continued neediness, and a heightened sense of neediness interferes with letting your husband go.

A word of caution on this point: Guard against excess in either direction. When do healthy preoccupations become unhealthy? When they, too, become obsessions. When your response to your aloneness is the frantic, helter-skelter pursuit of outside activities in an attempt to fill up the void within you. I refer to this as the flight phase; it is not an uncommon occurrence. Still, our goal is balanced emotional living, and excess in either direction is to be avoided.

Utilize Substitute Behavior

When giving your husband space, you are to limit your contact with him. I find this to be a difficult task for many women. The need to hear his voice seems especially strong at night.

"I'll just give him a call. I won't ask him to come home . . . or whether he loves me . . . or if he's changed his mind. I won't tell him I miss him . . . or that I can't stand being by myself . . . or that I love him. I'll just talk to him for a while. What harm will that do?"

When the emotional pull to have contact with him is this strong, it's good to have a long list of friends you can call. Go ahead and pick up the phone. But instead of dialing his number, substitute that of a friend. Make sure the friend is aware of your need to have someone to talk to in times like this. She needs to know what you need from her. By substituting a friend for your husband, you are able to continue your goal of backing off, you reduce the frustration that would have resulted if you actually had talked with your husband, and you reduce your level of neediness.

If you want, you can even substitute the entire behavior. Whenever the desire to call becomes almost unbearable, use that as a cue to walk a mile or do something else physical. Do anything but call him! For substitute behavior to work best, your plan of action needs to be set in advance. It's difficult to be creative in the midst of an emotional crisis. Predetermine what you will do when you have your next "attack." Then all you have to do is execute the substitute behavior.

Develop a Support Network

Receiving emotional support from others at a time like this is extremely important. Don't fall into the isolation trap. Sitting at home will only make you miserable. Even though you may not feel like being social, it is important that you socialize and actively involve yourself with others.

I'm really talking about two different areas here. First there is socialization in general. This is where you take part in some fairly superficial group activities. Clubs, parties, and small gatherings of friends are all examples of ways you can break the isolation cycle. These gatherings need not be large or formal. The important thing is that you remain socially active.

More important than this general aspect of socialization, however, is your need for some significant emotional support. This is nonsuperficial in nature and comes from true friends. They need not number in the masses, but they need to be close and highly supportive. These are people with whom you can share your hopes and dreams as well as your fears and pain. They are approachable, available, and accepting. They care, and they allow you to be yourself. In short, they are your true friends.

I have also found a formal support group to be extremely helpful in times of separation. These formal support groups are composed of ten to twelve individuals who are going through a separation. The group is led by a professional therapist who understands your particular needs and what's in the best interest of your relationship. It's amazing how much bonding is created by having a common pain. Members frequently utilize the group telephone list to seek or give emotional support. Informal get-togethers subdue your tendency to withdraw.

Remember, whether it is in the form of superficial socialization, in-depth friendships, or formal groups for emotional support (or a combination of all three), your goal is to stay active. You do not want to become isolated. Your control over troublesome emotions increases as your support network becomes established.

Study Questions

1. As the separation continues you may be faced with the normal emotions of neediness or anger. Write down the details of how you are going to take control of troublesome emotions.

2. How will you focus on yourself?

3. How will you be involved in healthy preoccupations?

4. How will you utilize substitute behavior?

5. How will you develop a support network?

Your Response

_____

_____

_____

_____

_____

_____

_____

_____

_____

_____

_____

_____

6

Troublesome Thoughts

Stacy was in the early weeks of a separation. Tim had unexpectedly left her for another woman. The early weeks seem to be the most difficult emotionally, but Stacy was beginning to recognize the difference between better days and worse days. It's always a good sign when the days start differentiating instead of just running together in one painful blur.

"I'm doing a little better. I can tell because there are some days when I even think that I might survive all of this. But those moments are short-lived. My mind keeps going back to Tim and what it was like to have him with me. We had so much fun together. *All those good memories really get me down.*"

Isn't that interesting? Rejected, abandoned, alone—and her thoughts keep going back to all those good times! Unusual? Not at all. In fact, this is fairly normal. All those good memories that Stacy was referring to, as well as many other forms of troublesome thoughts, are part of what interferes with a wife doing what she needs to do. They really have a way of demoralizing a wife when she is separated from her husband. In order to be able to do what needs to be done, these troublesome thoughts need to be handled. They do not need to be allowed to interfere with a wife letting her husband go.

Thoughts from the Past

Past thoughts are always haunting in nature. You think back on all the things you could have done, should have done, or even should not have done. Then you beat yourself to death with them.

- It was all my fault.
- I should never have. . . .
- I could have done better.
- I could have done more.

Talk about making yourself feel guilty! These will do it.

Past thoughts are also selective in nature. Stacy provides us with a perfect example of this: "All those good memories really get me down."

Most relationships have those good memories. But interspersed with the good times are the bad—the disappointments, the hurts, the frustrations, the little idiosyncrasies that make us unique but slightly irritating. Where are these memories? For a time, they are forgotten and overpowered by all those good times. Haunting, selective recall like this causes a great deal of grief for a wife contending with marital rejection.

Thoughts of the Present

Present thoughts are always frustrating in nature.

"It's so unfair. It's easy for him but hard for me. It's just not fair for him not to suffer the way that I am." That kind of thinking would tend to make you very angry. Anger is natural and normal, but you need to control it, rather than allowing it to control you. Sometimes thoughts can fan the flames of anger so strongly that the task of retaining control is made very difficult.

"We shouldn't be separated. It's not right. We ought to be working on the relationship." What usually follows this sequence of thoughts is the following: "Surely I can reason with him. If

I just say the right things—or say them enough—I'll convince him, and he'll come back."

You can see where this scenario is going. Frustrated with the situation, and now convinced that all she has to do to get her husband back is to talk to him, this wife will abandon the let-him-go philosophy and once again pursue him, pushing him further and further away in the process.

Of course, we cannot leave out the troublesome thoughts of a wife who has put her husband out. "I don't want to hurt him. He's so pitiful." What kind of interference do you think this will prompt?

Thoughts for the Future

Troublesome thoughts regarding the future always paint it as bleak and dismal. For instance, some thoughts project the present into the future. We think life will always be like this. "I'm going to be poor for the rest of my life. I'm going to be alone for the rest of my life."

These types of thoughts come with interchangeable parts. All you have to do is replace the descriptive adjective in the sentence and you can continue making depressing statements about your future all day long. For example, you could also use the words *miserable, lonely,* and *depressed.* Whatever it is that you are presently experiencing gets projected into the future. "I will *always* be this way or in this circumstance."

Some other thoughts in this category revolve around the issue of stigma.

- I'll be labeled a divorcée.
- I'll be a marked woman.
- They'll call me a single-again.
- I'll become a statistic.

There is also a fear of what the future will hold if their husbands do not return.

- All the good men are already taken.
- I'll have to deal with dating and sexual games again.

Finally, with a shaken confidence in their own ability to make good judgments, there is fear that they will never know what is right.

- If my husband returns, will I ever be able to trust him again?
- How can I ever be sure, after making a mistake like this, that it's a right decision to marry again?
- Will I ever be able to trust another man?

The fear of being able to make a correct decision or of being able to trust again is very real. They were so sure about their first choice—and look what happened. What's to prevent the same thing from occurring in the future? And if they cannot trust a man, there is no potential for intimacy. Without intimacy in their relationship, they will only continue to feel alone, and the thought of this is intolerable.

Troublesome thoughts come in a large variety of shapes and sizes. However, whether they be haunting memories from the past, frustrating thoughts of the present, or apprehensive thoughts for the future, they all share one thing in common: They all have an uncanny ability to interfere with the productive behavior of an abandoned wife.

How Troublesome Thoughts Interfere

Remember, your goal is to let your husband go. You are working toward a healthy reconciliation by taking control of your life and allowing him some space. You want the marriage to remain intact, but you cannot force your husband to stay. He has to resolve whatever it is that has motivated him to leave before he will be truly ready to work on the marriage. We know all of this. Then how do troublesome thoughts interfere with this occurring? Quite simply, thoughts similar to those just described encourage wives to pursue their husbands.

Let me explain the difference between the direct and the indirect ways these troublesome thoughts encourage wives to pursue. An example of a direct relationship would be this thought: "We shouldn't be separated. It's not right. We ought to be working on our relationship. Surely I can reason with him. If I just say the right things—or say them enough—I'll convince him, and he'll come back." There is an obviously direct course of action suggested by this line of reasoning, but that course of action is nonproductive.

While it is fairly easy to see how this thought can interfere with the behavior of a wife intent on letting her husband go, many troublesome thoughts have a far more indirect nature. Take, for example, the following thoughts: "It was all my fault. I could have done more." These thoughts from the past elicit strong feelings of guilt. Look at some more examples: "I'm going to be alone for the rest of my life. No one will ever find me attractive again."

These thoughts for the future serve to exacerbate the already present feelings of isolation and neediness. We discussed in the last chapter how troublesome emotions can interfere with a wife doing what she needs to do. Now we see that an indirect way in which troublesome thoughts interfere with letting a husband go is by serving as an enhancer of those already prevalent troublesome emotions.

The human makeup is complex. We are not simple creations. One way of looking at man is through the eyes of the cognitive behaviorist. He sees man as thinking, feeling, and acting (behaving). Even this attempt at explaining human complexity is too simple, for there are obviously many factors (family history, life experiences, value systems, biological factors, and so forth) that influence personality development, thinking, feeling, and behavior. Still, for the sake of understanding the indirect manner in which troublesome thoughts can influence the behavior of a separated wife, this cognitive-behavioral model has importance. Note the following diagram:

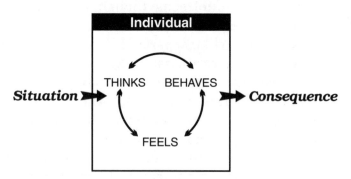

The individual is represented by the box in the center of the diagram. Complexly, he simultaneously thinks, feels, and behaves. Although theorists differ on which of these three elements is the most important and the order in which they occur, most agree that they function interactively. In other words, each influences the others. How I think influences how I feel and what I do. How I feel influences what I do and think. What I do influences how I feel and what I think. The individual is constantly encountering situations to which he must respond; he is always in a context of circumstances. Once processing the situation, he responds. This always leads to consequences— the results of his response.

The point is this: Troublesome thoughts indirectly interfere with letting your husband go by influencing how you feel. When your natural feelings of despair, neediness, and anger are exacerbated by what you are thinking, your ability to behave correctly is made much more difficult.

The problem is clear. Whether the troublesome thoughts represent direct interference or indirect, they need to be reduced if the task of letting your husband go is to be accomplished.

Thinking Straight

Changed thinking will not make a bad situation good, but our aim is to deal appropriately and directly with reality. I have found the following tactics to be helpful in taking control of troublesome thoughts.

Determine What Is Factual

Some degree of irrationality is normal during times of extreme crisis, and marital separation definitely qualifies as a crisis. But just because irrationality is normal doesn't mean we don't need to deal with it. Challenging irrationality by determining what is factual is a means of reducing troublesome thoughts. For example, it is normal to have a series of thoughts like these: "My husband will never come back. I'll never survive the loss. I'll be alone the rest of my life." But are these factual? Are they statements of truth? Let's see.

"My husband will never come back." Is this factual? No. At least, we cannot say that he will never come back. We know he is currently choosing to be out of the marriage, but we don't know that he will never return. Part of our goal of letting him go is to enhance the possibility that he may return. But there are no guarantees either way, so saying that he will never come back is irrational and should be replaced with a more rational alternative, such as: "My husband has left. I don't know whether he is going to return or not. He may. But regardless, I am going to do what is in the best interest of myself and my marriage until things resolve themselves one way or the other."

What about this thought? "I'll never survive the loss." Is it factual? No. We know you are in extreme emotional pain now, but this cannot be projected into the future. If your husband does choose not to return, you still can't say that things will never get better. In fact, we do know that most people survive the loss, make healthy adjustments, and get on with their lives. They do survive. A healthier and far more rational thought would be something like this: "I am in a great deal of emotional pain now. And I know it will be difficult if he chooses not to return. But I will survive. I will feel good again. There will be happiness once more in my life, although there may be a little time before I feel fully healed. Things will get better." This is not only a thought that is conducive to calmness, it's also accurate.

What about the final thought in this scenario? "I'll be alone for the rest of my life." Is this factual? No. Once again, we cannot predict the future. But there are two things we do know. First of all, a secondary thought accompanying this is the idea that if she is alone for the rest of her life, she will be miserable. Actually, this isn't necessarily the case. Paul stated that he had learned to be comfortable in whatever state he found himself (see Philippians 4:11). Most adults who are "seeking first the kingdom" can attest to the same finding. We are adaptable people. There is meaning to life outside the marital relationship. Singleness may not be the status of choice, but it is far from a miserable condition.

The second challenge to this thought is that the great majority of those who do divorce eventually remarry. Most divorced women do not proceed through the rest of their lives in a state of singleness. Obviously, this thought is not factual. A more accurate line of reasoning would be the following: "If my husband and I do divorce, there is a chance that I will remain single. But the odds are far greater that I will remarry— even though I don't feel much like doing that now. Even if I don't marry again and remain single, I know I can find happiness by myself also. God always has a future for His people, and a future with God, even without a man in my life, is good."

Again, the goal here is not to deceive ourselves. The situation is not good. But neither is it disastrous. We need to challenge the thoughts that bombard us and determine whether they are factual. If they are, then we need to deal with that reality. But if they are not, we need to recognize that and replace them with more accurate thoughts that truly represent our situation. We will find these to be far less troublesome to deal with.

Recognize the Kickers

Sometimes it's not the primary thought itself that is irrational or troublesome, but a parenthetical "kicker" that tags along. Here are two statements that will serve as examples. The first statement is factual and rational. Although not desirable, it can be faced and dealt with. The second statement, however, represents an irrational kicker. It overlooks the factual nature of the first thought and inflames the situation. "If my husband does not return, there is the chance that I will go through life alone. That would be unbearable!"

See the influence of the kicker? It acts as an incendiary device, igniting what in and of itself is a fairly factual thought. Kickers deal with extremes. They push things out of perspective. They are words like *terrible, disastrous, unsurvivable.* Quite frankly, a situation may not be good, but few things are truly terrible. If we tell ourselves that something is that extreme, however, we often believe it.

When dealing with troublesome thoughts, it is important to get out the *whole* thought. Make sure that there are no unrecognized kickers tagging along with what you're telling yourself about the situation. If there are, they need to be challenged. Remember, your goal is to deal with reality, not an exaggerated point of view. Reality is difficult enough. Exaggerated aspects only become more troublesome.

Do Not Project the Present Into the Future

The present is bad enough without imagining that that's the way the rest of your life is going to be. Feeling alone, upset, frustrated, and angry—being rejected, criticized, discounted—these may be an actual part of your present reality. But they need not be a part of your future. Thinking they will be is simply not factual. I cannot predict exactly what your future will hold, but I can guarantee that it will not be what it is now. Things will be different. They will change.

Your marital situation will change. Now you are separated, in a state of marital limbo. That will not persist. You will either move toward reconciliation or you will move toward marital dissolution. Either case will represent a change in status, and both denote a getting on with your life—resolution in one form or another.

Your emotional state will change. Being in a marital crisis, you are naturally upset. But that will change. Your emotional system will not allow you to remain in that kind of tension indefinitely. For your own protection and survival, your emotional state will change. We talked before about the attachment that takes place between a husband and wife. When this emotional bonding is interrupted, it prompts anxiety and emotional upset. You remain this way until one of two things occurs. Whatever is interfering with your attachment may be resolved, thus allowing you to be emotionally close again (genuine reconciliation). Or you will gradually disengage (emotionally pull away) from your husband until your attachment is totally severed. When there is no bonding, there is no pain. In either case, your emotional state will have changed and you will be out of pain.

Your life situation will change. You will either reconcile with your husband and resume a different married life, or you will enter the world of the formerly married. Either way, you will move from the chaos that totally engulfs your present life to something a little more stable and, hopefully, a little more sane.

These are just some of the changes that will occur. The important point to recognize is this: What's happening now is not your destiny. Things will get better—one way or another.

Do Not "Resist" Troublesome Thoughts

I had a client who complained that she could not get thoughts of her husband out of her mind. It seemed as though every waking moment was spent thinking about him.

"I'm obsessed with this separation. I can't work, take care of the children, even talk to friends. I'm constantly thinking about Tom and what he's done."

I asked my client what she had tried to do in order to reduce this obsession. This was her response: "I resist the thoughts. Whenever they come to my mind, I try and think about something else or I tell myself, 'I'm not going to think about this anymore.' But it doesn't seem to help."

Ironically, this was a case where the solution actually became the problem. Thoughts concerning an estranged husband, whether they be good memories or assessments of what he's doing now, are fairly normal in situations like this. They're disconcerting, but they usually pass unless we do something to make them an ever-present part of our existence. That's just what my client did. In an effort to eliminate thoughts of her husband, she only increased his hold on her. Telling yourself not to think about something is tantamount to telling yourself to go sleep when you have insomnia. The mental activity involved in telling yourself to go to sleep usually keeps you awake. My client's solution to resist her thoughts actually became the problem by holding onto the thoughts and preventing them from naturally dissipating.

If you have recurring thoughts about your husband, don't fight them. Go ahead and think them. If they are irrational, correct them. Some particularly troublesome thoughts may require special attention. Set aside some time to do nothing but concentrate on them. After twenty to thirty minutes are up, go on about your day. You'll find that those nagging, obsessive thoughts will gradually diminish.

Be Honest about Your Past

It is amazing how we tend to gloss over the marital history in times of crisis. I referred to this earlier when discussing thoughts from the past. Remember how the wife used selective memory when thinking about her relationship with her husband? She could only recall the good times, none of the bad. This is a fairly common phenomenon.

When plagued by thoughts of what it might be like if your husband chose not to return, be honest with yourself. Try to keep a realistic perspective. Ask yourself, "Was it really that good?" If it was, you probably wouldn't be in the situation you're currently in. I'm not suggesting that you make your husband totally the villain. I've seen too many marriages to believe this is the case. But instead of being haunted by the good memories, recognize that there were also some bad aspects of your relationship and that it was probably a cooperative venture. Your husband had a role in the marriage's deterioration, and if all you can hope for in reconciliation is to get things back to the way they were, you still may not have too much.

Call a Friend

You will recall that one of my suggestions for dealing with troublesome emotions was to develop a support network. That's all I'm suggesting here. A great time to utilize this network is when you are being bombarded with troublesome thoughts. Call or meet with a true friend—someone who understands what you're going through—and ask her to help you think straight. She can help you sort through what's factual and what's not; where a kicker is really exacerbating your thinking; where you're projecting the present into the future; where you're fighting too hard to avoid some painful thoughts; and where you're not being honest about your past. In short, friends can help you take further control of your life. With their help, you will be better able to let your husband go.

Study Questions

1. Write down the thoughts that trouble you in the three following areas:

   Thoughts from the past (i.e., I should never have . . .)

   Thoughts of the present (i.e., It's so unfair . . .)

   Thoughts for the future (i.e., I'll be labeled a divorcée . . .)

2. How do you think the troublesome thoughts listed above have interfered with a possible positive outcome of the separation?

3. What concrete steps will you be taking to rid yourself of recurring troublesome thoughts? (Remember the guidelines in the chapter—What is factual?, What are your kickers?, Projecting the present into the future.)

Your Response

7

Sexual Issues

Sexual issues between mates who are separated are always a problem. Should they remain sexually active or shouldn't they? Can they continue to sleep together? These questions, coupled with a myriad of mixed emotions, create general confusion regarding the entire area of sexuality.

My position regarding sexual contact between mates during a separation is that it is undesirable. I see no positive gains coming from it. On the contrary, it interferes with any possible reconciliation. Continued sexual activity serves to maintain fuzziness in the relationship, as opposed to clarity. You'll recall that I said you need to structure the separation—*clarify* it. Part of successfully letting your husband go is defining the rules and roles of the separation to eliminate any fuzziness or confusion. Continuing to be sexually active with your separated husband doesn't do this; it promotes haziness. When you're separated, you're separated. There is to be no sex.

Second, continuing a sexual relationship with your husband helps maintain his comfort zone, thus distorting the reality of what he has done. He thinks, "Being separated isn't so bad. I've got my own place. I come and go as I please. I do what I want, when I want. And I have 'all the comforts of home' when I want them. This isn't bad at all."

A major goal of backing off is to remove your husband's comfort zone. You want him to experience reality, to see what it's like to be on his own. Continuing to be sexually active interferes with this goal. He isn't fully experiencing the consequences of his actions and isn't in a position to resolve

119

whether he wants to remain in the marriage or leave it. You want him to make this decision, so you shouldn't reduce his discomfort. He needs to experience the stress that comes from being alone, and this is hardly accomplished by continuing to be sexually active.

Sexuality between separated mates usually emerges as a problem through one of three issues, one or more of which will certainly be a problem for you at some point during your separation.

"I Can Win Him Back with Sex"

Characteristics
With this particular mind-set, you approach your husband as the pursuer. This kind of behavior is best described by the attitude "get him back any way you can." Frequently, this advice from friends encourages you to pursue him sexually. To say the least, this form of behavior is manipulative and doesn't reflect honesty and emotional health. It is the desperate act of a desperate person.

How It Occurs
Wives can pursue their husbands sexually either passively or actively. Let me illustrate the differences in these with two case examples. I had been counseling Mary for about three months after Walt left her. Although he claimed he had been frustrated with the marriage for years, there was some evidence to suggest that he was being pulled out of the relationship. Mary was having difficulty letting him go. She said that she needed to be married and thoughts of living alone were devastating. Walt had not yet resolved what he was going to do regarding his marriage, and it was time for the family's

annual vacation, so he suggested they all go to Florida for a week, just as they had done for the previous two years. Mary quickly consented. Walt saw this as an opportunity for "painless convenience," nothing more. Mary, on the other hand, saw this as a chance to win him back. She bought a number of new nightgowns, all of which were designed to entice Walt.

"I'm not going to throw myself at Walt. But I'm definitely going to be available. After all, we will be together for a week. I don't think it will take much to interest him. And I want to make sure he knows what he's going to be missing if he gives me up."

A more active means of sexually pursuing a husband is illustrated by Lucy. She, too, desperately wanted her husband to return, but Ted had not yet resolved his reasons for leaving. Rather than passively pursuing Ted, Lucy set a trap. She prepared a nice candlelight dinner for two and surprised Ted when he brought the children home from a day of planned visitation. How could Ted refuse? With the children in bed, Lucy proceeded to serve Ted dinner and ultimately convinced him to spend the night.

Whether passive or active, both types of sexual pursuit are basically the same: Out of desperation, a wife manipulatively pursues her husband in an attempt to win him back. Both approaches interfere with letting him go.

Consequences for the Relationship

What are the results of this kind of behavior? What are its consequences? Does being sexually active move you toward success? To answer these questions, you have to examine your goals. If your goal is to have occasional sexual encounters with your husband, then you could argue that this form of behavior is successful. However, if your goal is for a genuine reconciliation and the fostering of a healthy relationship, then you have to answer that this pursuing and manipulative behavior is definitely unsuccessful. Continued sexual activity during a separation will not restore a marriage. It will not get you what you want. Pursuing behavior, whether sexual or in any other form, is never effective.

Not only will it not result in the restoration of your marriage, it also interferes with your doing what you need to do. You can't let your husband go and sleep with him at the same time. Being sexually active with your husband sabotages the let-him-go philosophy and plan of action.

Consequences for You

We can see that being sexually active with your husband will not restore your relationship, but what will it do for you personally? How will it make you feel? Will it benefit you or hurt you? In one word, it's bad for you. It damages your self-respect. Let me illustrate what I mean with the following diagram:

REASON or MOTIVATION

	Right	Wrong
Right		
Wrong		

BEHAVIOR

All human behavior can be placed somewhere in this diagram. Sometimes we do the right thing for the wrong reason; other times we do wrong things for right reasons. Our goal is to do the right thing for the right reason. Although this will sometimes bring us into conflict with those around us, it is generally the most productive way to live with others. Regardless of the external consequences it may precipitate, doing the right thing for the right reason definitely adds to our internal calm. We are dealing here with issues of personal integrity. When you do the right thing for the right reason, you feel good about yourself. When you deviate from that portion of the diagram and move toward the other areas, regardless of the category, your self-respect begins to diminish.

I view sexual activity during a separation as wrong behavior. But even if you wanted to argue that point with me, there's no denying the fact that it's wrong motivation. Anything performed manipulatively is wrong. As such, this kind of activity damages your self-respect. Even if you were successful in winning your husband back, you would not feel good about it. Since you probably won't win him back like this, you'll end up feeling even worse. You can't win; the consequences of this type of behavior are always bad. To feel good about yourself, you have to do the right thing for the right reason.

What You Need to Do

There are two things that need to be done if you are going to deal with this particular form of interference successfully. First, you must resolve the issue of "I can win him back with sex" by rationally realizing that this will not get you what you want. You want a reconciled marriage, not a one-night stand. Reconciliation is your goal, and that never comes through manipulation. This fact must become a truth for you.

Second, you must continue to back off and let him go. Don't be sexually available. Don't actively manipulate him by setting a sexual trap. Be honest and direct. Follow through with your goal-directed, prescribed plan of action. Take a stand, clarify the separation, remove the comfort zone, and let him go.

"I Owe It to Him"

Characteristics

With this particular mind-set, your husband approaches you. He may be swinging out of the relationship, but he's more than willing to swing in sexually. When your husband pursues you in this manner, there are two things that motivate you to respond to his demands: confusion and fear.

Confusion is represented by the thought, *After all, we are still married.* Frequently this is the advice of some of your well-meaning friends. If not, you can bet it will be firmly stressed by your husband. In your confused state, unsure of what's right and what's wrong, you consent to his request.

Fear is represented by the thought, *If I deny him, he may decide to never come back.* You may come up with this fear all on your own, or, once again, it may come with a little help from your husband. "I was thinking about the possibility of coming home. But you're blowing any chance of that happening right now. It's clear that you don't care anything about me." The ploy of "you're blowing it" is effectively utilized by husbands in many situations, but it usually comes up in regard to sex.

How It Occurs

To Brittney's total surprise, her husband came home from the office one afternoon and announced that he wanted a divorce. Within a week, he had rented an apartment, taken part of the furniture, and nearly dropped out of sight. She was still reeling from the unexpected separation when he "dropped by" to pick up a few more of his clothes. Discovering that the children were visiting friends, he suggested they go to bed together. Brittney was stunned and surprised. How could he suggest such a thing in the midst of this emotional chaos?

But she desperately wanted him back and feared what her refusal might prompt him to do, so she consented. She hoped this was an indication of his desire to return home, but it wasn't. His quick frolic was matched by an equally quick departure as soon as he had gotten what he came for.

Consequences for the Relationship

Does responding to your husband's sexual demands aid in the restoration of the relationship? No. Just as with trying to win him back, responding to his initiative for sexual activity will do nothing to get what you want. It only aids in keeping him away. You are failing to let him go and interfering with the clarification of the separation.

Besides all of that, it has been my experience in situations like these that you can never do enough. There is the implication in your husband's threat ("If you don't, you'll blow any chance of my coming back") that if you do as he requests, he *will* come back. Women who have succumbed to this manipulation report that this does not occur. They give and give while he takes and takes, but apparently they can never give enough. He just continues to make demands and do as he pleases.

Consequences for You

As with the previous category, the consequences for you personally are bad. Responding out of confusion or fear leaves you with a residue of emotions—all of them damaging to your self-esteem. You feel used. It doesn't take long to realize you've been manipulated, and with that realization comes anger. You feel gullible. "How could I be so stupid? How could I let him treat me that way? What was I thinking about?"

Add to this a feeling of worthlessness and you can see why Brittney was so devastated. Responding out of confusion or fear only results in further rejection and damage to an already shattered self-esteem.

What You Need to Do

There are three things that need to be done if you are going to deal with this particular form of interference successfully. First, you must resolve the question, "Do I owe it to him?" Once you have genuinely answered this question for yourself, your course of action is clear. From my perspective, the answer is no, you do not owe sex to your separated husband. In reference to the issue of responsibility, don't be confused. He has left; separation means separation. Even though you are still married, your relationship is temporarily "on hold"— and so is your sex life. In reference to the fear that not giving in to his demands may push him away, this is only manipulative behavior on his part. Even if your acquiescent response did result in his return (which it won't), what would you have? A relationship based on threat and intimidation is not worth much. As you can see, my answer is no. However, you cannot function on my answer alone. You must resolve this question for yourself.

Second, you must state this resolve to your husband. You must clarify the separation. Rather than passively dodging the issue, you must make him aware of the new rules. He must know what you will and won't do. Make him aware through declaration.

Finally, you must follow through with your plan and end the cycle represented by the old rules. Your husband will not like your declaration. He will argue with you. He will try to convince you that you are wrong; that you are not fulfilling your wifely responsibilities; that you are ruining what little chance there is for the two of you to get back together. Don't be swayed by his manipulation. By being resolved and understanding his game, you will be able to resist pressure of this kind. If you feel that you may not be able to resist his manipulation, ask a friend to be present when you have to be in contact with your husband. Do whatever it takes to follow through with your resolve to not be sexually active and establish the new rules.

"I Need It Myself"

Characteristics

With this particular mind-set, either one of you could be the initiator. You could approach him for sex, even though it wouldn't be with the goal of manipulative gain. On the other hand, he could approach you. If you consent in this situation, your response is not based on confusion or the fear of what rejecting him may mean for the future of your marriage. The motivation for this kind of sexual activity is far more basic. It's the practical problem of your own sexual desire—a desire that is often heightened by feelings of emotional neediness that are prompted by his departure.

How It Occurs

Whether you are the initiator or the responder, the desire for physical pleasure or emotional closeness seems to trigger this form of sexual activity. The sexual relationship was designed for our pleasure. We can talk all we want about how our culture has used and abused sex, but that doesn't change the fact that its original intent was for our good. Although many have found it to be mundane or even distasteful, many others have had very positive sexual experiences during their marriage. Their desire for this does not change merely because their husbands have temporarily chosen to leave the relationship.

I remember talking with a client regarding this issue. I was searching for some deep motivation that prompted her to maintain the sexual relationship between herself and her husband. After probing for a few minutes, I finally asked her directly. "What is it that keeps you going to bed with Tim?" She paused for a moment, smiled, and then responded, "You mean, besides the fact that I enjoy it?"

Sometimes we get so caught up looking for psychological motivations that we lose sight of some very obvious possibilities. It is very difficult to give up something from which you derive a great deal of physical pleasure.

But need and pleasure extend beyond the merely physical plane. When we are lonely, we frequently look to sex as a means of obtaining a feeling of closeness to someone—even when this someone has hurt us very badly. As another one of my clients remarked, "The loneliness outweighs the pain that he has inflicted on me. Sometimes I just feel so empty that I have to be with him."

When you feel emotionally needy or desire the physical pleasure that you used to experience, you are the most vulnerable to this form of sexual threat.

Consequences for the Relationship

In my opinion, this type of behavior only interferes with your goal of letting your husband go by maintaining fuzziness. Are you separated, or aren't you? This type of confusion is counterproductive. Second, it prevents your husband from dealing with reality. He thinks he wants to be out of the marriage, but he is not certain, so he has left to determine what he wants. Is it better out there or back home? How will he find out if he never has an opportunity to experience life without you? Swinging out of the marriage and still maintaining a sexual relationship at home is not experiencing reality. Husbands need to experience the real world—to determine whether those greener pastures are all they are cracked up to be. Don't help him hang onto his indecision; let him deal with the real world—alone.

Consequences for You

If trying to win your husband back with sex depletes your self-respect and responding to his sexual advances out of confusion or fear leaves you with a damaged self-esteem, then what are the personal consequences of maintaining a sexual relationship because of your own personal need? Once again, you're the loser. I repeatedly hear the regrets of wives who are caught in this cycle. Never do I hear their praises.

"I am miserable each time after we have sex. I tell myself that I'm not going to do that again. I'll be stronger next time. But I'm not. He calls, I feel needy, and I reach for whatever closeness I can get. It leaves me feeling inept and weak. I feel so out of control of my own life."

Women who maintain a sexual relationship out of their own need always feel demoralized as a result. To use my client's words, they feel weak. This feeling only adds to their other feelings of failure and helplessness. Is there any wonder I view this as bad?

What You Need to Do

There is a naturalness about this aspect of dealing with sexuality during separation that complicates the situation. I find it easier to deal with the issues of manipulation, confusion, and fear. We are sexual beings, and this fact cannot be changed, but we don't need to allow this fact to give way to license. We have always been faced with the need to control our sexuality, and "extenuating circumstances" do not absolve us of our responsibilities in this area.

What I have to offer as suggestions, therefore, are not total solutions. They will not cause your sexuality to disappear. Rather, in acknowledgment of the extenuating circumstances, they are meant to serve as aids to help you in dealing with your problem.

Sexuality is physical, but it is also far more. It ties together emotional aspects of our being and represents one dimension of intimacy in relationships. That is why loneliness will often heighten our normal sexual desires. We want to be close to someone—to be intimate—and making love with them is one way to achieve this. If loneliness heightens our desire for sexual closeness, then one means of diminishing its effect is to remain socially active. The key here is socialization versus isolation. Don't become socially isolated. Spend time with other people. Your emotional support network can be especially useful here. This will not eliminate your problem, but reducing your feelings of isolation by developing and maintaining intimate social relationships with concerned friends can definitely aid in taking control of a seemingly overwhelming problem.

Another suggestion is that you develop some physical preoccupations. Our health-minded society offers many options for you: running, walking, swimming, tennis. It's best if your choice is something that is both physical and interesting to you. It's hard to keep doing something you don't enjoy. Being physically active on a regular basis will help release some of your pent-up frustrations. It won't make you nonsexual, but it will help you control your desires.

Study Questions

1. Take the following three ways some spouses convince themselves to continue the sexual relationship with their estranged mates and write, in your own words, why these arguments are both spurious and faulty.

   - I can win him back with sex.
   - I owe it to him.
   - I need it myself.

Your Response

_____

_____

_____

_____

_____

_____

_____

_____

_____

_____

_____

_____

8

Ploys and Manipulations

If you are separated from your husband, you must expect and learn to deal with several possible forms of ploys and manipulations. One motivation for manipulative behavior is clearly selfishness—the overt desire of a husband to have things his way. The other motivation for this type of behavior is to satisfy his own emotional neediness or his dependency on you.

What is manipulation?

> *To manipulate:* manage by clever use of influence, especially unfair influence.
>
> *A manipulation:* a change for one's own purpose or advantage.

As these definitions make unmistakably clear, the goal of manipulative behavior is to gain advantage, to benefit oneself at another's expense. It is neither honest nor considerate of your need, but purely self-satisfying. It is one problem with two different motivations, but regardless of the motivation, the goal remains the same: advantage for himself at your expense.

The case of Angie and Jeremy offers us a clear example of a husband's ploys and manipulations. I never met Jeremy. Although he and Angie were still living together when I became involved with their situation, Angie had already filed for divorce. She and Jeremy were still living together because he refused to move out of the house. For Angie, twelve years of harassment had taken its toll. She was resolute—she had made her decision: In the interest of her sanity and that of their children, she had decided to dissolve the marriage.

Angie described a relationship marred with many incidents of abuse (both emotional and physical) and frequent accounts of unfaithfulness. Jeremy had behaved selfishly throughout the entirety of their marriage, and his abusive acts were aimed at maintaining control of Angie's behavior, thus allowing him to do as he pleased. He would inflict her with bodily harm, threaten to divorce her and leave her penniless, and constantly berate her appearance and competency as a mother and homemaker. Secure in his domination at home, Jeremy would then run with his friends and become involved with one woman after another.

What struck me most about Angie at our first meeting was her calm, tranquil appearance. In the midst of marital chaos, her demeanor was anything but frantic. I attributed part of this tranquility to the fact that Angie had made her decision, but I also guessed that some of her control was merely a cover. Some people have an uncanny ability to project an exterior that is quite different from their interior. I asked Angie why—if things were as bad as she described—she had waited twelve years before trying to take control of the situation.

> I tried to leave Jeremy once before. We had only been married for three years then, and we didn't have any children. I was afraid of what he might do if he knew my intentions, so I didn't say anything about my plans. One day after he left for work, I packed my bags and went to a friend's house.
>
> Jeremy literally came unglued. He found out where I was and came over in a rage. He demanded that I return home. I refused. This only made him madder. I don't know what he would have done if there hadn't

been witnesses present. But he finally left in a huff, making all kinds of threats if I didn't return right away.

After a few days he began to call on the telephone . . . except now he was very apologetic. He admitted that he had mistreated me. He didn't know why—but he would make it up to me. He was a changed man. We could have a good marriage. My leaving caused him to realize just how much he loved me. He begged me to come back, but I refused. I told him I needed time to think.

Jeremy grew more desperate. He called and threatened to kill himself if I didn't come home immediately. I refused. I later got a call from his parents. Jeremy had taken an overdose of sleeping pills and was at the hospital. He was okay, but the doctors wanted to watch him for a few days. They pleaded with me to go and see him at the hospital and to end this "foolish separation."

I felt so guilty—so responsible. I agreed to see Jeremy at the hospital. We had a long talk and, once again, he assured me that he was a changed man. So I agreed to move back. Things were good for about two weeks, and then it was right back to the way it was before I had left.

I began thinking about leaving again and then discovered that I was pregnant. I began to get concerned about security. What would I do with a child and no husband or job? I got scared. So I decided that I could live with things as they were for a while longer. At least, I could stay until I got through the pregnancy. That was nine years ago. It's hard for me to believe I've spent another nine years in that situation—nine years in misery.

Those nine years had not been totally uneventful. Angie became pregnant again, so now she had two children instead of one. Jeremy had climbed the corporate ladder. Even though he controlled all the money, a divorce settlement would leave Angie with some financial security. But most importantly, Angie had gone back to school and was on the verge of graduating. This had been done, I might add, with a great deal of resistance from Jeremy. But the result was greater autonomy for Angie. She was now in a position to begin a career of her own, thus making her far less dependent on Jeremy for her financial security.

You might be wondering why Angie came to see me at all. Her mind was made up. She was getting a divorce. What need did she have for a therapist? Divorce is never easy, and even in extreme situations like Angie's, leaving is difficult. There are always adjustments to be made. Also, she still feared Jeremy and his power to manipulate. She needed a coach, someone who could decipher what was going on and keep her moving in a healthy direction. I was her choice.

We had only been seeing each other for a few weeks when her need for a therapist became evident. I knew something had happened. Angie's cool, calm, and collected demeanor was gone. She appeared rattled. "What's the matter?" I asked her.

> Jeremy has filed for custody of our son. He's been fighting the divorce all along. At first he said he would change and be a better husband. You know, all the things he said the last time I left. When that didn't work, he said he'd never support me. He'd go to jail before he'd pay any child support. He would quit his job. I'd starve to death. Now he says he'll take my son away from me. I'm scared. I think he really means it. I don't know what to do.
>
> Jeremy has never been a father to our children. If anything, they've been a burden to him. I have to usher

136

them out of his way when he is home, and he's constantly complaining about the noise they make. Jeremy still ignores our daughter, but now, all of a sudden, he's trying to be the ideal father to our son. He bought him a baseball uniform and glove, takes him to ball games, buys him anything he wants, and tells him they're going to live together when I leave. It's a competition. He's trying to buy his affections, and he may succeed.

Surely, Jeremy doesn't love our son. I don't think he loves anyone but himself. But the thought of him getting custody of our son terrifies me. I'm an emotional wreck. I just don't know what to do.

If you have been following this story closely, you recognize that this attempt to get custody was merely one in a long list of ploys and manipulations executed by Jeremy. My question to you at this point, however, concerns his motivation. Was Jeremy selfishly attempting to gain control of Angie to have things his way? Or was he responding from his own emotional neediness, his excessive reliance on Angie for emotional completeness—his dependency? Actually, he was behaving manipulatively for both reasons; he was motivated by selfishness *and* emotional dependency. The following diagram will help us clarify the situation.

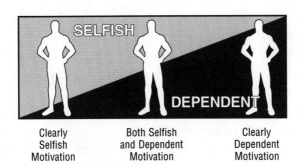

| Clearly Selfish Motivation | Both Selfish and Dependent Motivation | Clearly Dependent Motivation |

The diagram on the preceding page illustrates just how these two separate motivations for manipulative behavior operate. Selfish motivations are represented in the portion of the diagram with the ▒▒ pattern, whereas dependency motivations are represented in the portion of the diagram with the ▆▆ pattern. As you can see, there are times when a husband's motivation will be either/or and he will be either clearly selfish or clearly dependent. There will be other times, as in the case of Jeremy, where his motivation will be a mixture of the two, selfish and dependent. Let me give you some examples of husbands with a singular motivation—those who are clearly either selfish or dependent.

An example of a selfishly motivated husband would be the case of Pam and Greg. When I first met with Pam she was in utter confusion. Greg had left her, reporting that he was unhappy with the marriage as it was. This was Pam's first indication of displeasure. Although Greg was suggesting that he was pushed out, there were many indications that he was in fact being pulled out. Greg's selfishness surfaced over what he wanted Pam to agree to during their separation. He did not want a divorce, at least, not yet. He stated that he was uncertain as to exactly what the future would hold for their marriage. However, he did want Pam to agree to a property settlement that he drew up and his attorney would make legal.

"I don't understand any of this. Why does Greg want a settlement agreement if he's uncertain whether he wants a divorce or not? I've read what he proposes, and it doesn't seem very fair. Can I trust his attorney to represent me, too? I don't know what to do!"

In situations like this, I always recommend that my client secure her own attorney. Greg's attorney may be a fine, honorable man, but when all is said and done, it is Greg he represents. Pam followed my advice. And what was Greg's response? He was incensed.

"How can you do this? You're just wasting money by procuring the services of a second attorney. Mine can represent you. If you follow through on this, you're throwing away every hope that I might come back. You might as well file for divorce. Do this and it's over!"

Greg's behavior was highly manipulative, and his motivation was purely selfish: He wanted to control the settlement. As things turned out, his property settlement proposal was highly unfair and there was someone else waiting in the wings. He had hoped to get a favorable settlement agreement and then file for divorce. But Pam, although confused by his strategy, did not give in to his manipulation. She did what seemed fair and appropriate—she procured her own attorney. She didn't strive to control Greg, only to take control of her situation and not be controlled by him. This she accomplished.

Barbara and Wally exemplify a clearly dependent motivation. Wally was being pulled out of his marriage. Barbara was an emotional wreck. She had already gone through the long and predictable list of pursuing behaviors before I first met with her, but this had not swayed his resolve to leave. Still, she continued to pursue. Barbara called Wally on the telephone twice a day, once at work and once every night before she went to bed. It never made things better. In fact, she always felt worse. Still, she kept calling. Having read this far, you obviously know that the first thing I did was put a stop to all forms of pursuing behavior, including the phone calls. Barbara issued her statement of declaration and then proceeded to let Wally go. And how did Wally respond to Barbara's backing off? He began to call her.

What a turn of events! Now, instead of Barbara hanging on, it was Wally. Of course, Wally had a reasonable rationale for his behavior. "I'm just calling to make sure that you're okay." But every attempt to have him stop his demonstration of concern was ineffective. He kept calling. When Barbara finally refused to take his calls, Wally accused her of being bitter and vindictive. Why else would she refuse to talk with him?

What was Wally's true motivation for calling? Was he genuinely concerned for Barbara's welfare? No, certainly not. As with all other forms of manipulative behavior, Wally's goal was to influence Barbara's behavior to his advantage. In this particular case, what motivated him were his own personal emotional needs. He was not genuinely concerned about Barbara, only about himself. Even though he was being pulled out of his marriage, he was not certain that the other woman was what he truly wanted. He still felt something for Barbara, and he needed her to pursue him or he would feel lonely. And loneliness was something that Wally could not tolerate. He used other people in order to feel good about himself. As Barbara pulled back emotionally and let Wally go, he became increasingly uncomfortable.

Telephone calls are one way dependency is manifested. There are others. For example, I have a client whose pulled-out and emotionally dependent husband moved into a new apartment, yet he found excuse after excuse to drop by the house every day. Sometimes it was to check on his wife. At others it was to pick up some forgotten household items. At still others, it was to see if any mail had failed to make it to his new address. What was his real motivation for coming by? Emotional dependency. He was doing it for himself; he was hanging on.

This is manipulation, one problem with two separate motivations. Sometimes manipulation is a case of either/or—clearly selfish or clearly dependent. At other times it is more a case of selfish *and* dependent. Regardless of the motivation, the goal remains the same: to gain favor for himself at your expense.

When it comes to dealing with this particular problem of marital separation, manipulative behavior always interferes with letting your husband go. It is hard to do healthy things when your selfish husband tries to control your behavior through threats and intimidations. It is equally hard to let your dependent husband go when he is feverishly holding on to you. The husband who mixes the two motivations—who controls and clings—represents just as clear an interference as does one who possesses the more singular orientations. Still, like all other interferences, manipulation can be dealt with. An interference may add more difficulty to your task, but it need not prevent you from accomplishing it. Manipulation can be handled.

Frequently Seen Manipulations

The following is a sampling of some of the more frequently demonstrated acts of manipulation that I see as a therapist. Some of these are clearly coercive while some are clear examples of false acquiescence, and others fit into neither of these categories. Regardless of the strategy or its motivation, please bear one thing in mind: The goal of any manipulative behavior is to gain an advantage over you at your expense.

"I Want Custody of the Children"
Sometimes this is a legitimate desire of a husband and father. Frequently, however, it's used to strike fear in the heart of a desperate wife. It becomes a bargaining chip. If you give him something he wants or do something he wants you to do, or stop doing something he doesn't want you to do . . . *then* he'll drop his suit.

"I Don't Have Food Because of Your Child Support"

The goal of this strategy is fairly obvious. What's different about it is that it's directed through the children. Not only is this behavior manipulative, it's also damaging to children. Whenever possible, children need to be kept clear of adult conflict.

"You're Playing Dirty"

This was the remark of a husband whose wife chose to get her own attorney rather than accept a settlement prepared by her husband's attorney. He had hoped to coerce her into changing her mind, thus placing him in control of the proceedings.

"You're Ruining Any Chance for Us to Get Back Together"

A very common ploy, this appears anytime a wife begins to establish some healthy boundaries in her life. Determining what you will and will not do, declaring it, and then enforcing it is usually viewed as resistance from a departing husband. It may be a refusal to talk with him, a refusal to remain sexually active, or a decision to retain your own attorney. It makes little difference; this strategy is good for all occasions.

"You're Vindictive and Bitter"

This was the statement utilized by one husband whose wife refused to talk with him more than once a week on business issues. In this particular situation, the wife had called her husband on a daily basis. When I got her to stop calling him, he began to call her. Of course, he claimed this was out of concern, but I suspected it was more out of dependency. At any rate, the results were the same for his wife. The conversations would end and she would be terribly upset. So we put a stop to the calls.

"I care about you and I care about our marriage. I have also come to realize that, whatever you decide to do, I will survive. But I find it very difficult to talk with you right now. It would be far better for me if we had only minimal contact and then only as it pertains to business issues."

The wife was trying to gain emotional sanity. What was her husband's response to this request? "You're vindictive and bitter. I only want us to remain friends during this ordeal. Can't you at least be objective?"

Actually, he wanted more than just to remain objective friends. He was hanging on, and didn't want the calls to stop, so he accused her of being vindictive in the hope of forcing her to resume telephone contact.

"I'll Change—Just Let Me Come Home"

This is the familiar statement of the put-out husband. Remember, his objective is to get back home at any cost. By acquiescing to his wife's demands and admitting he was in the wrong, he hopes she will allow him to return. But genuine change is not really on his agenda. When dealing with put-out husbands, you always have to hold out for demonstrated behavioral change over time. Promises are no good.

"If You Pressure Me, I'll Be Forced to Get a Divorce"

With this strategy, "any pressure" takes in the entire waterfront. This strategy is used by a husband who has left the marriage, probably for another woman, but who has not yet resolved whether he really wants a divorce or not. In order to gain some time to think, he threatens to file for divorce if there is any pressure placed on him whatsoever. "You may force me to do something that I don't want to do." What about child support, house payments, or structuring the separation? That is considered pressure. This manipulation holds a wife in limbo, and that's an uncomfortable position to be in.

"I'll Cut Off Your Money"

This overt coercion takes many forms. It's highly selfish, but may also be mixed with dependency. Other variations of this may be, "If you don't do what I want . . ."

- I'll beat you up.
- I'll harass you at home.
- I'll cause you to lose your job.
- I'll kidnap the kids.
- I'll kill myself.
- I'll vandalize your car.
- I'll destroy your reputation.
- I'll ruin your credit.

The list goes on and on. I've heard every one of these, plus others equally intimidating. What is the goal? To manipulate a situation to personal advantage.

"I'm Home, but I Won't Talk about It"

Let's pretend it didn't happen. Maybe this husband has a history of walking out when angry and then unexpectedly returning. Or maybe he had an affair that soured. At any rate, he has returned, but he does not want to deal with the incident. There is the implication that if you try to deal with the incident, he won't stay. The problem is, if you don't deal with the incident, he might as well leave. Without a genuine reconciliation, there will be no healing in the marriage. But will the fear of his leaving again manipulate his wife's behavior?

"I'll Come Back on My Terms"

Similar to the last manipulation, this husband also wants to avoid dealing with any real issues in the marriage, and he's counting on his wife's desperate condition to allow him to control the supposed reconciliation. A variation of this would be, "I'll come back, but only if you make some changes." This was the statement made to one of my clients by her husband when his affair ended. He was relying on his wife's emotional desperation to gain control of the situation and relieve himself of personal responsibility for the marital failure.

"It's Your Fault"

Placing a wife on the defense is a good strategy for gaining control of a situation. Already feeling guilty, she is very vulnerable to accusations. This is not to say that there may not be room for criticism, but seldom is one person solely to blame for a marital failure. I once heard this argument used by a husband who wanted to come home before his wife was ready for him to do so. He told her it was her fault that they were separated. "You should have tried to stop me from leaving." Some of the accusations are a little more convincing.

- You never cared for me the way you should have.
- You were never affectionate enough.
- You never understood me.
- The children were always more important to you than I was.
- You drove me to having my affair.

Sometimes these ploys are used to justify a husband's departure, but frequently they are to gain advantage through weakening an already damaged self-esteem. Once in control, he can have things his way or return with greater ease.

"Can't We Still Be Friends?"

This is the classic theme of a husband who is hanging on. He covers his dependency with noble gestures. He calls because he's concerned. He drops by just to make sure everything is going okay. He keeps in touch because "the least we can do is remain friends." Ironically, the very last thing a wife needs right now is a husband who wants to be friends. In reality, his concern is only a ploy. Noble intention is not his goal. His behavior is self-satisfying. He is leaning, he needs her, and he covers his dependency with noble gestures.

Dealing with Ploys and Manipulations

Ploys and manipulations are problematic. Being particularly vulnerable due to your present circumstances only adds to your difficulties. As one client so aptly put it, "Had I not been so vulnerable at the time, I probably would have handled things differently. But I wanted to believe him. Even though everything he was doing contradicted what he was telling me, I was too blind to see it."

The effectiveness of ploys and manipulations can be hindered. Whenever you are dealing with manipulative husbands, bear these things in mind.

Keep Your Blinders On

Blinders are the flaps that force a horse to look in only one direction—forward. They prevent him from seeing objects at his side. When dealing with a manipulative husband, you must remain focused on your goal—what's in front of you—and not be distracted by your husband's various ploys. What is your goal? To let him go.

What does focusing on the goal mean for a husband who is dependent? It means you have to sever his attempts at hanging on. If he frequently calls you on the telephone just to talk or because he is concerned, you need to structure the separation.

"I'm going to survive. There's no question in my mind about that. But it is difficult for me right now, and I find it

146

much easier when we don't talk together. So I would appreciate it if you would not call me anymore."

So you have told him not to call, yet he persists in hanging on. Now what do you do? You escalate. "I've asked you politely not to call. I told you it's difficult for me to talk with you right now. If you persist, I'll have no recourse but to hang up when I find that it's you on the phone."

Still, he persists. He even starts making accusations that you're acting out of anger, are bitter, and are behaving vindictively. Don't be swayed. Remember your goal. "I am angry about what is happening. Who wouldn't be? But that's not why I'm doing what I'm doing. I'm not being vindictive. But I do have to do what is in my best interest in this situation. So do not call me."

After that, don't continue to discuss what he considers a problem. It will resolve nothing. His goal is not resolution—it is to stay in contact. Just follow through on what you said you would do. Hang up when he calls.

What does focusing on the goal mean for husbands who are selfishly trying to control your behavior? It means you have to resist his maneuvers as you continue to do what is in your best interest. If what little chance there was that he might come back is "going out the window" because of something you are either doing or not doing, tell him, "I'm sorry if that's the way you feel, but I have to do what I believe is right in this situation. I do not want a divorce. But if that is what you choose to do, there is little I can do to stop you. You will have to be responsible for your decisions as I will be for mine."

When his manipulation involves intimidating threats, whether they are the withholding of needed resources, harassment, or actual physical violence, you have to impress upon him that you do have legal recourse and that you will not fail to exercise it.

"If you don't do as I say, I'll stop giving you any money at all for child support."

"I do not wish to take legal action. But to protect my children and myself, I will file if necessary."

"I'm going to come over and beat some sense into you."

"If you attempt to physically harm me, I will press charges."

Cool, calm, and collected. You need to be goal directed. You are letting him go by taking control of your situation and doing what is in your best interest, and any attempt on your husband's part to divert you from that goal needs to be handled directly. He must realize that you will do what is right regardless of what he says or thinks. You will take responsibility for your decisions and he will be held accountable for his. He will have no more power in this situation—no more control over you—than you allow him to have.

Don't Take Any Wooden Nickels

The goal of letting a husband go is to get him back through genuine reconciliation, but living together and reconciling are not necessarily the same thing. It is possible for a husband to want to return home without a genuine reconciliation. To accept a husband back when his intent is not for genuine reconciliation is tantamount to accepting a wooden nickel—something of false value.

The situation involving the put-out husband is the most obvious. He will predictably promise anything in order to be allowed to return home. But this strategy should be seen as the manipulative ploy it is, and handled accordingly. Put-out husbands must meet a number of legitimate prerequisites before being allowed to return. At the very least, they must demonstrate changed behavior over an extended period of time. To allow a put-out husband whose repetitive irresponsibility has warranted a separation to return on a promise to change is to enable him to maintain his pattern.

His initial goal is to *not* change. He wants back, but he wants things as they were. Regardless of his promises, do not take this wooden nickel.

Another wooden nickel would be a husband returning totally on his terms, where his terms are that you do not deal with the relationship. Possibly his affair has soured and he thinks you are desperate enough that he can come back home and pick up where he left off. "I don't want any questions, hassles, or arguments. I don't want to talk about it. Let's just forget it ever happened and get on with our life."

His affair may have ended, but there is no suggestion of a true swing back toward the marriage in this type of maneuver. With the absence of true remorse, there is no opportunity for genuine reconciliation here. It is a clear example of selfishness. The husband is returning for his own welfare and no one else's. There can be many variations of this "returning on my own terms," but bear this in mind: All of these are wooden nickels!

The manipulation and motivation of these two situations are fairly obvious. A more subtle wooden nickel is represented by the husband who, although uncertain about what he wants to do regarding his marriage, wants to come home and deal with his confusion. "I'm not sure what I want to do. Sometimes I think the best thing to do is get a divorce. But I know I still care for you. I just don't know what I want right now. I can't make any commitments, but I want to come back home."

Frequently this type of response is a demonstration of dependency, not an indication that any of the motivation for leaving has been resolved. This husband finds being on his own uncomfortable and, even though he is not genuinely swinging back toward the marriage, being at home is seen as more desirable than being on his own. Do not accept a husband back under these conditions. It is just another wooden nickel.

Part of letting him go is to force him to deal with reality. Only by allowing this to happen will some husbands "come to their senses." This is often an uncomfortable and anxious experience, but for some, it needs to be. Allowing an uncomfortable and confused husband to return would not only interfere with his coming to grips with himself but would prove frustrating for you as well. Living with him in his confused state day in and day out would literally frustrate you to death. During this time of marital crisis, you must do everything possible to bring stability to your life. Accepting a husband back under these conditions would only add to your chaos. Until there is a firm commitment to your marriage as an institution, and an agreement to work on your marriage as a relationship, any suggestion of returning home should be rejected.

Ask for Help
Dealing with ploys and manipulations is difficult. You want to do the best thing, but your husband's maneuvers, whether motivated by dependency or selfishness, can definitely interfere with your constructive attempts at letting him go. Because of this, it is frequently helpful to seek out the aid of a qualified third party, someone who can coach and advise you how to relate to your husband during this time of crisis. This third person need not necessarily be a professional marital therapist, although this may be the ideal. Whoever you choose, he must be approachable, available, and sound in his judgments. In the midst of manipulative forces competing for your attention, you need someone who can keep you focused on your goal, who can aid you in letting your husband go. In short, you need someone who can keep your "blinders" on.

Don't be afraid to ask for help. These are difficult times. Find someone who is qualified to assist you, and then work together toward your goal.

Study Questions

1. Have you, or has your spouse, used any of the following ploys and manipulations? If so, describe what you feel is the strategy or motivation behind the ploy.

    - I want custody of the children.
    - I don't have food because of having to pay child support.
    - You're playing dirty.
    - You are ruining any chance of us getting back together.
    - You are vindictive and bitter.
    - I'll change—just let me come home.
    - If you pressure me I'll be forced to get a divorce.
    - I'll cut off your money.
    - I'm home but I won't talk about it.
    - I'll come back on my terms.
    - It's your fault.
    - Can't we still be friends?

2. Are there any other actions by either you or your spouse that could be seen as manipulation?

3. How would you deal with manipulation? Use the following guidelines to plan your reactions to ploys that could be, or have been, used against you.

    - How do I focus forward?
    - How do I discern "real" promises from "convenient" promises?
    - Whom can I go to for help and support?

Your Response

9

Extended Family and Well-Meaning Others

Family members and friends can offer much-needed emotional support during times of separation. However, the focus of this chapter is on interferences, not aids. Even though there are many ways in which family members and friends can offer aid in times of emotional crisis, there are also things they can do that interfere, and it is these interfering activities that we'll discuss here.

Tendencies of Extended-Family Members

His Family

The following case illustrations are intended to represent a variety of situations involving in-laws. They move from one extreme to another; you determine where you fit into the continuum.

CASE 1: Ann and Fred

Ann's mother-in-law never accepted her. Fred had been "petted" all of his life, and when it came time for him to marry, there was simply no one good enough for him. At least, this was his mother's perspective. Ann had to take a tranquilizer every time they went to Fred's parents' home, just to survive the visit. When Ann finally put Fred out for repeatedly abusing her physically, her mother-in-law encouraged him not to return. She openly supported her son's behavior, claiming that Ann deserved what she got and taking every opportunity to ridicule her as a wife. "She's never been good for you. I don't know what you ever saw in her, anyway. If she were half a wife, she wouldn't have kicked you out."

CASE 2: Betty and Greg

Betty's mother-in-law outwardly approved of her, stating that she was the daughter that she never had. She had two children, both boys, of which Greg was the younger. But in spite of this outward show of affection, Betty had always felt more a rival than a daughter. "Throughout the entirety of our married life, I felt as though Greg's mother was competing with me for his affection." Apparently Greg's father had invested most of his emotional energy into the life of Greg's older brother and Mom compensated by investing in Greg. When Greg left Betty under suspicious circumstances, both his parents told Betty that they hoped things would work out between them. But instead of cautioning Greg about hastily pursuing a divorce, they immediately gave him the money he needed for filing. Betty took control of her life and began setting expectations for the marriage, which included counseling, should Greg wish to reconcile. When Greg suddenly had a change of heart and wanted to return home to Betty, both his parents encouraged him to go ahead with the divorce. "Don't stay in the marriage. Get on with your life. You don't need her."

CASE 3: Cathy and Henry

Cathy's mother-in-law treated her as one of the family and stated she was the best thing that had ever happened to her son. They lived close enough to be neighbors and were frequently in contact with one another. All this changed, however, when Henry left. Although he was fairly discreet, it was no secret that Henry was being pulled out of his marriage. An old rekindled flame with a woman from Henry's past had prompted him to leave his marriage of twenty years. Cathy's mother-in-law's initial response was one of anger. "How could he do such a thing?" But she allowed him to move in with her anyway. It was not long, however, before her resistant support became more overt.

"She actually covers for him. I call late at night trying to reach him and she tells me he's playing golf or just stepped out. I know on two of those occasions that he was out of town with his girlfriend. How can she treat me this way?"

CASE 4: Dee and Larry

Dee had what she thought was a good relationship with her mother-in-law. In fact, it appeared to be better than that between Larry and his mother. Larry had lived a fairly protected life-style while growing up, and Dee continued the tradition. Larry's involvement with drugs had exasperated his mother. Now that he was a married adult, she frequently found herself in sympathy with Dee's difficulties with him. She was resoundingly supportive of Dee's attempts to get Larry involved in rehabilitative help for his addiction, but their united effort was never enough. Larry refused to succumb to their pressure. As Dee became less enabling of Larry's drug addiction and began establishing a life for herself within the marriage, Larry decided they should get a divorce. Both he and Dee seemed ready for the dissolution. Remarkably, calmness seemed to be the order of the day. Although saddened by the situation, even Larry's mother was acceptant of what was about to occur.

"Larry has certainly blown it. I know that it's probably best for you this way, Dee. But it's a sad occurrence for Larry."

Dee and Larry worked out what seemed to be a fair and equitable settlement. They had no children, so all that was involved was the division of personal property. Everything was proceeding smoothly. Suddenly, on the eve of their court date, who should appear but Larry's mother. She had reverted back to her old role of rescuer.

"You can't agree to this property settlement. You're giving Dee way too much. It will put you in a tight spot. Fight this thing."

So Larry did as his mother suggested and, due to the laws of that particular state and the prevailing attitude of the local judiciary, Dee ended up with very little.

CASE 5: Ellen and Jack

Ellen's in-laws were appalled by their son's behavior: "We're not going to condone sin. We don't know what's come over him." Jack had left Ellen and their teenage daughter for another woman. He came from a deeply religious family. All his brothers were pastors, and his sisters had married pastors. His father was president of a Christian college. Even Jack had been in Christian work for a while. No one understood his behavior, no one condoned it, and everyone asked him to change. But he refused.

Still, Jack was his parents' child. And even though they were genuinely supportive of Ellen, their strong parental ties could not help but come through. In this particular case, the ties didn't emerge as a condoning of Jack's behavior but as discouragement of Ellen's taking control of her situation. It was permissible for Ellen to condemn Jack's behavior, but only as long as she patiently (and martyrfully) waited for the prodigal's return. Any effort to force him to assume responsibility for his actions was met with a cool response.

"We understand how you feel, but can't you give him a little more time?"

It made little difference that Jack had been living with another woman for over a year and that every effort to talk with him about the situation had been rejected. Neither did it seem to matter that his financial behavior was as irresponsible as his personal life. With lavish spending and increasing indebtedness came Jack's refusal to provide any financial support for Ellen or his daughter. Although Ellen was not really emotionally ready to force the issue in the courts, three months of no money forced her to do so. She felt she had no alternative; she had to protect herself and her daughter. What was the response of her in-laws to this decision? "We understand your situation. He is in the wrong. But couldn't you be just a little more forgiving and wait a little longer? Surely he'll change if you just keep holding on."

I've often wondered what would have been the response of Jack's parents if the situation had been reversed. Would they have championed long-suffering if Jack were the one holding the home together and Ellen were the one living in adultery? Probably not.

These five examples represent a full spectrum of responses, any one of which can be expected from your husband's family members. Did you find yourself in any of them?

Continuum of Support

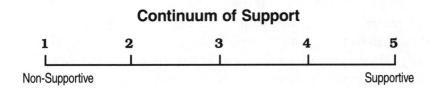

Interestingly, although these examples moved from one extreme to another, they all had a common theme: *Blood is thicker than water.* This is always the case.

A family member's behavior is predictable. Even though my focus in these illustrations has been with mothers-in-law and fathers-in-law, the theme is not limited to these roles. It also includes aunts, uncles, brothers, sisters, and so forth. Sure, there are occasional exceptions, but not many. Basically, family members align themselves according to bloodlines. Regardless of how good a relationship you have with your in-laws, or how bad your husband's behavior, you can expect an alignment according to family ties. It may take a while for this pattern to clearly show itself, but it will. Your goal is to be prepared for this inevitability.

Your Family

If blood is thicker than water in your husband's family, it's even more so in yours. After all, he's the rejector and you're the rejectee. He's the one behaving irresponsibly, and you're the one trying to hold the marriage together. Recognizing that emotional support is an aid during this time of crisis, why do I view this as an interference?

The emotional and tangible support of family members during a time of marital turmoil is very helpful and needed. But it becomes an interference if they begin to influence your decisions.

Janie's husband left her, claiming he was no longer interested in either Janie or the marriage. They were just too different to get along. It would be better for both of them if they divorced and went their separate ways. He saw their differences as irreconcilable. Janie was initially devastated by Ken's announcement and rejection but gradually regained emotional stability as she took control of her life. Her plan was to give Ken some time. Even though he said he wanted a divorce, he had no real grounds. For a quick divorce to occur, Janie would either have to agree to a no-fault divorce or sue him for divorce on grounds that he had abandoned her and his two children.

As could be expected, Janie's parents were very supportive during this entire ordeal. If a divorce were to occur, their home and financial resources were at Janie's disposal. More tangibly, Janie's mother immediately filled in and helped with child care. She was an ever-ready baby-sitter and picked up the children at the day-care center when Janie had to work late. To this point, Janie's parents' involvement could be described as supportive and viewed as good. Their over-involvement came as they tried to influence Janie's decisions regarding Ken. Ironically, even this influence was changeable.

Remember, Janie was trying to give Ken some time. She was attempting to follow a let-him-go plan of action. Her parents saw Ken as a cad, and their first suggestion was that she divorce him.

"If he doesn't want you, then you don't need him. How could any man abandon his wife and two children? He's not worth fretting over. Divorce him and be done with the whole matter. You could never trust him again, anyway."

This pressure made it difficult for Janie to do what she felt best. It also made it difficult to be around her parents. Ironically, as a little more time went by, their advice changed. Their suggestion was still motivated by the same dislike for Ken, but now it was for Janie to pursue a different course of action. "Don't give him a divorce. That's what he wants. Make him suffer. Drag it out as long as you can. He deserves all the grief you can give him."

Obviously, both positions espoused by Janie's parents were reactions, not actions. At a time when Janie needed to be making clear, goal-directed decisions, advice of this nature was an interference. This is the kind of family support that must be guarded against.

Tendencies of Well-Meaning Others

Well-meaning others are the friends and not-so friends who emerge to give you advice during a time of marital separation. It's always amazed me how many advice-giving friends a person has at times like this. Some may not have said as much as two words to you during your entire lifetime until this point, but now they know exactly what you should do.

Often the advice of well-meaning others has religious overtones, which makes it even more confusing. Just remember that all that glitters is not gold and all that sounds religious may not be. Even if it is sound religious advice, the motivation behind it may be less than pure. Furthermore, the multiple factors that complicate some situations relegate what frequently might be a sound suggestion in one situation to an inappropriate action in another.

As an aid in sifting through some of the advice you'll receive from well-meaning others, I have developed this characterized list of the most common ones. See how many of these friends have already shared their knowledge with you:

Saintly Sue

"It's not God's will for divorce. Don't lose faith and give up. We're going to pray that God will bring him back. You just have to believe."

Martha the Martyr

"I know what you are going through. I have lived with the same thing for forty years. I just keep holding on for things to get better. I know how miserable you are, because I am, too. But you have to hold on."

Sweet Sally

"Just keep loving him. That's the solution. If you are just sweet enough and keep giving, he will finally come back. Let him know what he is missing."

Desperate Doreen

"Do anything it takes in order to get him back. Anything!"

One-in-a-Million Millie

"My husband did the same thing yours is doing. I held on, didn't pressure him, just kept loving him. He finally came back, and now we have the best marriage anyone could want."

Righteous Rick

"You have to work it out. The Bible is clear on your responsibility in a marriage. It's your responsibility to hold things together. Your husband is still the head of the home. No matter what he does, God hates divorce and will hold you responsible."

Submissive Sam

"You're under your husband's authority. You must submit to him. Take him back on his terms."

Past Pensive Pauline

"Are you sure you've done everything you could do? I remember some things you could have done better."

Foreboding Florence

"Can you live without him? How can you handle everything alone? Who'll help you with the kids?"

Most of the well-meaning others listed above have offered advice aimed at keeping the two of you together. Here are a couple of friends who will offer suggestions representing the other end of the spectrum:

Good Riddance Gertrude

"Thank your stars and bars. You just got rid of two hundred pounds of ugly fat. You ought to be thankful he left. You are better off without him."

Cautioning Cathy

"Are you sure you want to let him come back? Can you ever trust him again? If he left once, he'll probably leave a second time."

As someone else has said, "With friends like these, who needs enemies?" Even though some of these well-meaning advice givers truly have your best interest at heart, their suggestions are still interferences. A true friend is one who will stand beside you and be supportive, no matter what. He may not always agree with the decisions you make, but he will agree with your right to make them.

How These Actions Interfere

Whether it be the alignments of family members or the well-intended advice of friends, these actions can have problematic consequences for a wife who is separated from her husband. These behaviors set off a chain of events that result in nonproductive behavior. Here's the interfering cycle:

It creates confusion, doubt, guilt, and frustration. You find it confusing when in-laws who had been close to you suddenly turn on you; when your own family members insist that you do this or that; when a number of friends offer you different advice. Already reeling from a blow to your self-esteem, you begin to doubt yourself even more, as well as your ability to make decisions. You even question your ability to assess the situation. You're already prone to feeling guilty, and now you feel both guilty and frustrated.

This prompts indecision and anxiety. As a result of the first step in the cycle, you become indecisive. "What should I do? What's right?" Indecision prompts a heightened sense of anxiety. You begin to experience a cyclical effect. Indecision creates anxiety, and heightened anxiety prompts greater indecision. They feed on each other until the cycle is broken.

Indecision leads to failure to follow through on a prescribed course of action. Indecisive wives don't take stands and they don't maintain the stands they do take. Indecisive wives don't let their husbands go. Indecisive wives don't remove comfort zones. In short, indecisive wives don't take control of their lives or aid their situations. They only contribute to an already difficult set of circumstances. All of this is partially the result of concerned family members and seemingly well-meaning others.

How to Deal with This Kind of Interference

Although there is little you can do to prevent some people from behaving in a circumscribed manner, there are things you can do to reduce the effects of these behaviors. I have found the following procedures helpful.

Realize It

Understand the rules by which people play. Blood *is* thicker than water, and there is nothing you can do to change this fact. It is normal, natural, and predictable. Likewise, it is just as natural and predictable for well-meaning others to offer you a wide variety of advice. Even if this motivation is based more on meeting their own personal needs than it is on aiding you, they will come out of the woodwork during your time of need.

Expect It

Don't be surprised. Plan on it happening. Be looking for it. This will lessen the impact when it actually does occur. I remember cautioning a client regarding her sharing confidences with her father-in-law. She insisted that he had been closer to her over the years than her own father. When she decided to take a little more financial control of her life by removing half of the savings from a joint account, she was surprised to find that her husband had beaten her to the bank, removed all the money, and placed it in an account in his name. Why was his timing so good? You guessed it. She had discussed her intentions with her father-in-law and he couldn't just sit there and watch this happen to his son. The moral of the story is this: Always expect a realignment to occur, and act accordingly. If it doesn't happen, so much the better, but you'll be the exception, not the rule.

Be Prepared for It

Since you expect it, be prepared for it. Be cautious regarding relationships with in-laws. I am not suggesting that you initiate any significant change in your relationship. However, you will need to be wary of your involvement and ready to make any needed adaptations. Likewise, when relating to your own parents, you will need to determine what you will and will not do. It is understandable that you will need to tread gingerly here; however, personal boundaries must be erected. You will have to take the lead in establishing exactly what role your parents can play in offering their support. The same is true regarding your friends and well-meaning others. You may even wish to have some of your responses prepared in advance. "I appreciate your concern, but I'm doing what I feel is best for both me and my marriage." Be cordial if possible. After all, we owe cordiality to everyone. But also be firm and resolute.

These suggestions will not prevent interfering actions from family members and friends, but they should greatly reduce their effects. Remember, your course of action is predetermined. You are goal directed. Working toward a healthy reconciliation, you are letting your husband go. As such, you are in a position to act, not react. This being the case, the behavior of family and friends need not interfere with your preferred course of action.

Study Questions

1. List all in-laws, other relatives, and friends who may be affected in some way by your separation. Identify from this group those who may attempt to interfere (out of either good or bad intentions).

2. Be prepared. Describe how you will deal with this kind of interference.

Your Response

_____

_____

_____

_____

_____

_____

_____

_____

_____

_____

_____

_____

_____

_____

_____

10

Vulnerability

There was an unusual lift in Trudy's countenance when she arrived for our therapy session—unusual in that she did not appear greatly distressed or discouraged. There seemed to be a spark of hope, a sense of anticipation in her. For Trudy and her situation, this was different.

I had known Trudy for approximately five months, since she knew for certain that her husband wanted a separation. From that time on, she seemed to move from one devastating blow to another.

Trudy reported that there had been nothing truly remarkable about her marriage, neither remarkably good nor bad. There were a few questionable encounters, but Trudy was always one to give the benefit of the doubt. So as things really began to deteriorate with Stan, she fought the thought that something was truly wrong until the last possible moment. Finally, she could deny it no longer. Stan's job-related traveling had increased over the past year and a half to the point where he was home only on weekends. The emotional tone in their marriage was poor, and their sex life had all but dried up. Then, all of a sudden, Stan announced he was going to rent an apartment in an area where he had most of his business accounts. He followed this with the statement that coming home every weekend was becoming too expensive. That was the last straw for Trudy.

"Okay, what's going on? I'm totally confused and really concerned about where this marriage is going. Is there something I should know?"

Stan was cool, calm, and distant. *Cold* would probably be a more descriptive term. "There's nothing going on other than work. But quite honestly, I haven't been happy with our marriage for years. I'm going to do what I need to do for my job. If you want to consider this a separation, go ahead. That's your choice. But that's not what I'm calling it."

Shortly after this encounter with Stan, Trudy came to me for counseling. Stan's intention to set up a separate residence, coupled with his voiced dissatisfaction with their marriage and his apparent lack of concern and caring for Trudy, were devastating. She was an emotional wreck.

Together, we chronicled the next five months, one event after another. There was Stan's failure to come home for Thanksgiving because of business. There was Christmas, and Trudy's ill-fated attempt to actively win him back with sex. Her sexual overtures were readily accepted, but her relationship was unchanged. The feelings of being used and abused, as well as her lowered self-respect, only made things more difficult for Trudy. Then there was the discovery of financial irregularities: loans with her name forged as co-signer, excessive and unexplainable entertainment expenses, rising debt, and the cessation of financial support. The culminating blow came with Trudy's discovery that there was another woman in Stan's life. For many months, Trudy had fearfully refused to face this possibility—a possibility Stan had steadfastly denied. But alas, the truth was eventually learned.

Things had gone from bad to worse, but Trudy pressed toward the goal of letting Stan go. She realized that this was the best course of action, whether he decided to swing back toward the marriage or not.

This was the state of affairs when Trudy came for her regularly scheduled appointment. I had expected to find her continuing to struggle through. Although "fighting the good fight," she would still be just surviving. But this was not the case. Instead of being anxious and dejected, she was calm and uplifted. She smiled. She spoke of the future, of things she planned to do for herself and her children. There was no obsessive preoccupation regarding Stan—life was bigger and better now. These were far different words than those of the week before. At our last appointment, there had been no tomorrow, only a continuation of the present—and the present was depressing.

Why the change? For months Trudy had been totally absorbed with her relational world, but not now. Now there were glimmers of hope. What had happened to cause such a change? This is exactly what I asked Trudy. And this was her response:

"I met someone this week. Someone who is kind, good, and caring. Someone who made me realize that there could be a future even without Stan. And someone who made me feel good about myself again."

Trudy went on to tell me every detail of this chance meeting, all the time assuring me that there was "no relationship," only an acquaintanceship. But she was exhilarated, nonetheless.

I arrived home from work to find my dog lying by the road. He had been hit by a car. I just fell apart. What next? Was my whole world going to fall into chaos? And where was Stan when I needed him? About that time Bill drove by. I must have looked real pitiful, because he stopped and asked if he could help. To make a long story short, he virtually took over for me. He got a quilt and picked up my dog. We then took him to the vet. Although he was still alive, the vet had to put him to sleep. I was still pretty upset, so Bill took me home and stayed awhile.

I told him how much I appreciated his help—how I didn't know what to do and how Stan had left me for someone else. He began to tell me about his unhappy marriage and how his wife is getting ready to divorce him. We seemed to have a lot in common.

As it turned out, Bill was visiting his mother. She lives a few doors down from me. He had to fly back home the next day but said he wanted to see me again. He enjoyed talking with me. He hadn't felt this good for a long time.

In five months of therapy, I had never seen Trudy feel any better than she felt during that session. She was definitely elated. But when I saw her a mere week later, she was once again depressed. In fact, she may have even been worse. Why the change?

"Bill hasn't called. It's been a week and a half since the day I talked with him. I haven't heard from him since he left. I thought he would call—I hoped he would. But I guess he won't. I'm so disappointed."

In this particular scenario, Trudy is clearly showing her vulnerability. Webster defines *vulnerable* as capable of being wounded and open to attack or damage (assailable). Although being vulnerable has its positive aspects (it's essential for a healthy and growing relationship), there are times when vulnerability takes on negative connotations. Choosing to be vulnerable in a relationship—to open yourself up, to share some of your normally protected self, to defy personal safety in the hopes of drawing closer to one you care about—is a positive venture. When our vulnerability emanates not from a position of strength, but from a condition of weakness, however, it becomes a liability, not an asset. This was the situation for Trudy.

Battered and beaten down, Trudy became tired, excessively needy, easy prey for others, and susceptible to affronts and disappointments. Being vulnerable caused her to act like a giddy schoolgirl over a man. Being vulnerable caused her to inflate this chance encounter beyond all bounds of reality. She saw him as a knight in shining armor sent to be her savior. Being vulnerable caused her to grasp this illusion as if it were her last hope. She needed him. And being vulnerable caused her to plummet back to the depths of despair when Bill didn't call and all hope disappeared.

The problem of vulnerability isn't unusual; it's a problem for most separated wives.

An At-Risk Group

Separated wives are an at-risk group: They share common circumstances that make them more susceptible to external influences. For example, infants who experience a premature birth are considered an at-risk group. As a result of their immature physical development, they are far more susceptible to diseases, developmental complications, and higher incidences of mortality than infants who are born at full term. Infants who have the advantage of reaching full maturity before birth have much less difficulty in dealing with those first few months of life. At-risk status is definitely warranted for the separated, too.

Members of at-risk groups are vulnerable. I must be careful, however, to differentiate between those women who have a *reactive* vulnerability and those who are vulnerable as a *way of life*. A wife who is reactively vulnerable is basically an emotionally healthy person. She's behaving momentarily in a vulnerable manner because of the extreme stress that has been placed upon her by the departure of her husband. She is reacting. A wife who is vulnerable as a way of life, on the other hand, is not as healthy emotionally. Although she, too, is experiencing stress from her husband's departure, she has a history of such incidents. Time after time, in relationship after relationship, she has been excessively needy. As such, she has been taken advantage of. Although the actions of these two wives are the same, a world of difference actually exists between them.

I find it helpful to determine very early in the therapy process whether I am dealing with a normal and predictable reactive vulnerability or whether it has been a lifelong state. A brief inquiry into a wife's relational history usually gives me a fairly precise and immediate indication. Let me illustrate with Kari.

At the age of twenty-five, and in her second marriage, Kari was already separated from her husband when she first came to my office. But it was not this marital crisis that finally convinced her to seek professional help. Rather, it was the occurrence of an unplanned relationship with another man that caused her concern.

Richard and I have been separated for three months. I guess it was only a matter of time. We've fought for most of our four-year marriage. He's so demanding. I thought that if I just gave enough, he'd change. But that hasn't worked. I tried to get him to go to marriage counseling with me, but he wouldn't have any part of it. I figured we both needed some time apart, so I moved out.

I started back to college to help occupy my time and to feel as though I were doing something constructive with my life. That's where I met Jeff.

I wasn't looking for anybody else. My life was complicated enough. But he invited me over to his apartment after class just to talk for a while. One thing led to another, and before I knew what was happening, we were doing more than just talking. Well, that was three weeks ago. I've been stopping by Jeff's apartment after class "to talk" twice a week ever since. I feel so bad—so out of control. It's as if I don't have any willpower. Why do I do this? How can I stop?

Kari is asking some good, difficult questions. Like Trudy, she is in a vulnerable position, but unlike Trudy, it is not solely because of the separation from her husband. Sure, this has served to exacerbate her emotional neediness, but by and large, vulnerability is a part of Kari's style of living. If Kari's present relational dilemma were to improve, she would still be left with a deeper problem. And unless this part of her personality changes, she will merely continue through life repetitively involving herself in unhealthy relationships.

Exactly why Kari is so vulnerable is difficult to say. Frequently (but not always), this type of problem has its roots in the family of origin. This was particularly true for Kari. There was something lacking in Kari's relationship with her parents; something was wrong with the way her family functioned. Although Kari learned to survive the craziness in her home, much of what she experienced as a child followed her into adulthood. The biblical admonition to put off childish things was difficult for Kari to do (see 1 Corinthians 13:11).

Kari's excessive need for love, her emotional neediness, the extent to which she would go in order to have her needs met, her unhealthy scripts or solutions—all these issues can be treated. But they are characteristics of a way of life, not merely a reaction to an event. The following diagrams will visually illustrate the differences between Trudy and Kari.

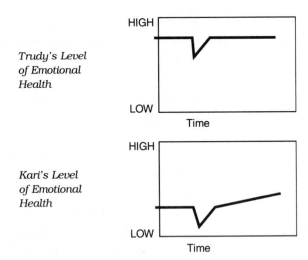

In Trudy's diagram, we can see that the stress created by the separation prompted a dip in her general level of emotional well-being. Although she is a fairly emotionally healthy person, the trauma was somewhat devastating. Given enough time and barring any unusual interferences, she should make an appropriate adjustment to her previous level of well-being. This would be our emotional goal and would be possible regardless of what happened to her marital relationship.

With Kari, a return to her previous level of functioning would only allow her to maintain an emotionally unhealthy life-style. Greater improvement is needed. Therefore, further intervention is required. The characteristics that underlie Kari's problems will not get better on their own. If improvement is made, it will be gradual, time-consuming, painful, and only after much concerted effort.

My only reason for taking a little side trip into this area is to differentiate between what's normal and what's not. Sure, there are many Karis in this world—many women who exist in a perpetual state of emotional vulnerability. But there are far more women who are emotionally stable but will predictably take on some unhealthy characteristics when rejected by their husbands. This is *normal vulnerability.*

You have been rejected; you are alone. Whether the abandonment has been for another woman, out of frustration, or due to the pursuit of irresponsibility, your self-esteem has been dealt a heavy blow. How do you react? You are devastated, needy, susceptible. You are part of an at-risk group. In short, you are vulnerable. You're normal, but you have problems.

The Problems with Vulnerable Involvement

A relationship that is the by-product of a weakened emotional condition is always bad for you. It may feel good for a season, but it interferes with personal growth and only serves to further complicate your life. Part of my reason for believing this is based on moral grounds, some is based on an understanding of basic psychological need, and still more is based on an awareness of what constitutes healthy relationships. All these factors point to the same conclusion: Although becoming emotionally vulnerable is a natural, predictable reaction to marital separation, having a relationship with another person is definitely not in your best interest. Here are just some of the reasons you should refrain from such an entanglement.

A False Feeling of Well-Being

Remember the elation felt by Trudy? She was on top of the world. Trudy's not alone in her reaction. I can cite many incidents where separated wives have responded similarly. One example would be Mary. Her husband had been pulled out by a co-worker at his office, but before he left Mary, he made some very cutting, devastating remarks. When her husband left, Mary went home for a visit.

"Going home was the best thing I could have done. I ran into one of my old boyfriends, and he made a pass at me. It was amazing. One suggestion from him dispelled a lot of myths. All of a sudden, I felt attractive and desirable again. I took the children to Florida the next week and really enjoyed myself. I hardly even thought of my husband. It was the boost I needed."

When we are in crisis, we are prone to look to external sources to bolster our own self-worth. This is true for even the healthiest of us. For a wife who has been rejected and feels she is no longer desirable, the interest of a third party can provide a definite boost to the ego. She suddenly feels better about herself, sees the future less bleakly, feels less alone, and has less desire to pursue her husband. As understandable as this may be, it is imperative that we recognize the deficiency of this sort of boost. It is tantamount to placing an adhesive strip on a deep wound—even though it may have the appearance of being helpful, the wound still needs stitches.

True self-worth comes from within us, not from without. It is how we view ourselves, regardless of the perspectives of others. To rely on the views of others for our own self-esteem is dependency, and this is unhealthy, regardless of the circumstances. Predictable, yes; healthy, no. We must strive to deal directly with the emotional pain brought about by the rejection and to feel good about ourselves on our own merits, instead of utilizing any artificial aids.

The Letdown Is Devastating

The emotional high experienced during an involvement precipitated by vulnerability is typically short-lived. Trudy's story more than attests to this fact. Some months after her brief encounter, we processed the event in one of our counseling sessions.

"Bill made things go so much easier for a week. I could let Stan go. Then he didn't call. Wow—did I ever bottom out then."

Jeanette, another client with a similar story, placed it in the present tense. "He hasn't called in a month. I'm devastated. This has been as painful as my husband leaving. It seems like no one wants me."

Disappointment in a relationship like this is almost a certainty. Whether you read too much into it or your situation is too complex, it will soon end. And when it does, all the false, inflated feelings of well-being that you derived from this fantasy will come crashing down like a ton of bricks. Ironically, even though this involvement has been much shorter in duration and probably far less intense than that experienced with your husband, because your vulnerable condition has predisposed you to experience pain more deeply, you will feel devastated. A relationship with a third party at this time is definitely not in your best interest.

You Make Poor Selections

In your better days—days when you weren't reactively vulnerable—you were able to make better decisions regarding men. You screened them pretty well. But now, in the midst of emotional devastation, your assessment skills have deserted you. Being alone and lonely has impaired your judgment. Instead of viewing men for what they are, you only see your personal need. You give them too much benefit of the doubt. More than willingly, you overlook obvious faults, red flags that would have previously prompted you to give them a wide berth. Instead, you attach yourself to people you normally would have avoided.

Val had a humorous way of describing her poor selection. This is what she said during one of my group sessions for separated wives:

"He was a scum bucket. Every quality that I normally couldn't stand, he possessed. Oh, he was bad. But I needed someone, so I overlooked all his obvious deficiencies."

Humorous, but sad. It never ceases to amaze me—the depths to which people will sometimes sink because of emotional need. Fortunately for Val, she was able to relate this as a past phase in her life. She went on to give a more successful ending to her story. "I needed someone then—but now I don't. I'm content to be by myself. I'd prefer to have someone in my life, but I don't need that kind of relationship."

In the midst of emotional crisis, you are not going to make good decisions regarding men. Your pain and your needs interfere too much with your rational self to allow this to happen. Poor judgments are the order of the day. You are far better off making no judgments at all.

It Complicates Decision Making about Your Marriage

This particular reason for avoiding these relationships is illustrated by a conversation I had with Mary. She discovered that her husband had been having an affair for over a year. When he was confronted with his behavior, he was not willing to give up the other woman. However, neither did he want a divorce. He didn't know what he wanted, so Mary put him out in the hope that he would resolve the relationship and become ready to work on restoring his relationship with her. In the meantime, Mary was feeling particularly vulnerable.

"I know I'm vulnerable right now," she told me. "But Bill's got someone else in his life. Why shouldn't I? Why should I be so lonely while he's trying to decide what he wants?"

I replied, "You need to be in a position to make sound decisions regarding your marriage. All that being involved with someone else right now will do is complicate your situation. For instance, what if you were involved in a relationship with someone else and Bill wanted to swing back into the marriage? What would you do?

"Here's another for instance. What if, through your involvement with another man, you decided you were ready to divorce Bill? I believe this would be a very poor basis on which to make such a decision. A decision of this nature needs to be made solely on its own merits. You really need to be out of one relationship before you enter another."

In order to make decisions regarding your marriage, you really need to be able to think clearly. There is more than enough unavoidable confusion during a separation, so why complicate the situation with things you can avoid? Do yourself a favor and don't add to your problem.

There Are Definite Moral Considerations

In most issues of living, there's a difference between secular and Christian standpoints. It's no different with the issue of marital separation. The world would tend to make statements like these:

- Your husband has left you. Go ahead and get involved with someone else.

- Your husband is involved with another woman. Why shouldn't you be involved with another man? Turnabout is fair play.

- You're separated. You don't owe him anything at this point in your relationship.

- If you're hurting, meet your own needs. That's what matters in life anyway.

Advice of this nature is plentiful, and if you listen to it long enough, it may even begin to sound right to you. But it isn't.

Just because your husband has chosen to violate his commitment to your marriage gives you no right to do the same. You are not responsible for what he does, but you are responsible for what you do. No amount of rationalization can change this fact. And as I have already stated, there is no right reason for doing the wrong thing.

Christians are destined to live in the world, but our calling requires that we be not of the world. From a Christian moral perspective, you are still married to your husband. Honoring this commitment regardless of his behavior is your responsibility.

There are other reasons for my belief in avoiding these entangling alliances: the tendency to get in over your head, legal ramifications, and the slowing of your adjustment. Involvements of this kind—as understandable as they may be—are definitely not in your best interest, so avoid them.

What You Need to Do

Let me make it clear from the outset that these suggestions are not intended to eliminate your vulnerability. Your humanity prohibits that from happening. You will feel very vulnerable. However, it's possible to deal with your vulnerability in a way that will prevent you from succumbing to temptations.

Maintain a Personal Spiritual Relationship with the Lord

Of all the suggestions, this is probably the most important. Nothing or nobody may remain stable in your life during this time of disruption. But always cling to the reality that God is constant. I have a plaque on my office wall to remind me of this fact. It reads: "In the beginning, God created order out of chaos. . . . He still does." You are indeed in the midst of chaos, but God can still bring order to your life. I don't understand all there is to know about the "all things" verses . . .

"Give thanks in all things" (see Ephesians 5:20).

"All things work together for good for those who love the Lord" (see Romans 8:28). . . . But even though I don't understand them, I believe them. What occurs may not be what you would have preferred. It may not be what He would have preferred. But in the midst of it, He is with us. As I stated in *The Drifting Marriage*, God always has a future for His people, and a future with God is always good.

Commit your situation into His hands and seek to draw nearer to Him during this time of chaos. Lean upon the Lord. Do not abandon Him merely because your husband has abandoned you. Experience His closeness and draw strength from His presence. This may be a time of unparalleled growth in your spiritual relationship.

Be Aware of Your Vulnerability

Recognize the normality of the problem and the probability that you will be plagued by it. It is only a matter of time. This may help prepare you to deal with potentially awkward situations.

Along with this realization, it is also good to visualize the costs of succumbing to your vulnerability: further disappointment, heightened confusion, and guilt that is associated with behaving in a manner inconsistent with your preferred lifestyle. Being aware of your proneness and the consequences may help you reject any hint of entangling alliances.

Resolve to Do What's Best for You

Before you find yourself involved in an unplanned relationship, commit yourself to not becoming emotionally entangled in any compromising situations. Choose to do what is right, not what feels good. Making a resolve of this nature and having a predetermined plan is a good preventative.

Act Early and Decisively

At the first hint of a problem, you need to act. Obviously, situations which even have the appearance of being problematic need to be avoided. But many of our compromising situations seem to occur with little or no advance warning. When this occurs, action must be taken early, before emotions become overwhelming. Any action you take must be decisive. I believe in this principle: Clean breaks are good breaks. If you are in a relationship that is leading toward further complication, break it off. Break it fast, and break it clean. Protect yourself.

Stay Connected to Your Support Network

Part of vulnerability is feeling alone and isolated. Even though some of this cannot be satisfied by relationships with good, caring friends, much of it can. To avoid feeling totally alienated, you must maintain contact with those who genuinely care about you.

I suggest that most, if not all, of your support network consist of women. This simplifies things for you. Also, I would suggest that you establish some regular times for getting together and not have it be totally an "as needed when I'm in crisis" arrangement. You may wear them out if you're in crisis every time they see you. They'll see you enough like this, anyway. Sure, you will need to have some who are available whenever you need them, but try to structure your social contacts as well.

Study Questions

1. Identify the areas in which you feel the most vulnerable (i.e., emotional neediness).

2. Describe the ways in which you will protect your current state of vulnerability.

3. What, in your opinion, is best for you at this time?

4. What decisive actions can you take now?

5. In what ways can you better stay connected to your support group?

6. How can you better maintain your relationship with God during this time?

Your Response

_____

_____

_____

_____

_____

_____

_____

_____

_____

_____

_____

Part Three

THE END
RESULTS

11

Husbands Who Want to Come Home

There are some individuals who would argue that there is no need for this chapter at all. Their rationale would go something like this: "Where's the problem? After all, isn't this what you wanted to see happen all along? Consider your mission completed . . . your goal accomplished. If he wants to come back, let him. And then go on with your marriage."

I only wish things were this simple. In reality, however, the complexity surrounding a husband's departure is only matched by his decision to return home. There is much more involved here than simply unpacking his suitcases. Remember, our goal is reconciliation, not just the resumption of an intact relationship. These can be two greatly different situations.

When separation occurred, only one decision was required—that of your husband. In fact, his decision to leave may have been met with much insistence on your part that he stay. Still, he left. His ability to return home, however, is much more the product of two decisions: his to return and yours to let him. You have a definite voice in whether he returns or not. It's not his decision to make on his own.

The exercise of this mutual power is made either easier or more difficult by legal restrictions, which vary from state to state, and the willingness of your husband to cooperate with your decision. But even in instances where there is no allowance for a legal separation and your husband insists on returning home when you are not ready for him, you could maintain the separated status of your marriage by moving to another residence yourself. Although this may be an extreme action on your part, there are times when it's called for. The point I am trying to make here is this: When it comes to the decision of reconciling a marriage, *two* votes are required, and both votes must be genuinely cast in favor of reconciliation.

Considerations

Making the decision to reconcile is not always an easy one. There are many factors involved. In an effort to aid you in determining how to cast your vote, I have listed four considerations that you need to evaluate. Applying each of these to your particular situation should provide some direction for your decision making.

Motivation to Return
Of utmost importance in considering reconciliation is determining exactly why your husband wishes to return. What is his motivation? There are appropriate and inappropriate reasons for the same behavior. Let me reproduce an earlier diagram to illustrate my point. (See opposite page.)

Every behavior has its motivation. Sometimes right behaviors are done for right motives. We consider these to be appropriate. At other times, however, right behaviors are done for wrong reasons. We consider these inappropriate. The key issue, therefore, is determining why you do what you do.

When it comes to dealing with marital separation and trying to restore a relationship, returning to a rejected wife is obviously a *right* behavior. However, it must be done for the right reason. Right reasons would include any or all of the following:

- Definite resolution of the motivation that prompted the departure in the first place.

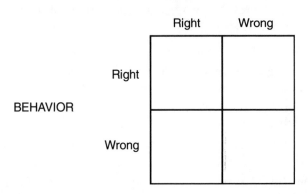

REASON or MOTIVATION

- A genuine desire to work on the problems in the relationship (this includes those problems created by the separation).

- A genuine remorse for the pain caused by the separation and a recognition of the need for forgiveness.

- A genuine acceptance of the personal role played (contribution) in the deterioration of the marital relationship.

- In the case of repetitive irresponsibility, demonstrated behavioral change over time.

There are also wrong reasons for returning to a marriage. In these cases, returning home would be an *inappropriate* behavior. Examples of wrong reasons would include any or all of the following:

- Personal loneliness yet having no real desire to be with the rejected wife.

- Purely logistical considerations such as needing a place to stay, financial strain, or personal convenience and comfort.

- Not attaining whatever it was that motivated him to leave

in the first place, yet also failing to resolve it (still has the "pull" to the other woman or the "push" of feeling trapped in the marriage).

- Needing to be in control of what's happening at home.

- Wanting to come back for any reason, yet being unwilling to deal with the relationship. "I'll come back if we can pretend it never happened [avoidance]. We can just pick up where we left off."

- Any reason that does not include acceptance of at least part of the responsibility for the marital failure and recognition of the need for forgiveness as opposed to blaming.

I feel very strongly about the need to differentiate between the appropriate and inappropriate returning of husbands. To endorse appropriate return is to place importance on genuine reconciliation. This provides opportunity for healing within the relationship. To endorse the inappropriate, on the other hand, is to place importance on intactness—the appearance of things being okay—rather than on true marital restoration. I have too frequently seen the results of settling for the appearance that all is well, and I find them greatly disappointing.

Take the case of Carl and Becky. After twenty-five years of what appeared to be a good, stable marriage, Carl left Becky to be with another woman, Susan. As the truth unfolded, their marriage had been stable for many years, but there were things Carl didn't like—needs he felt were not being met. What did he do? Nothing. Being a nice guy, he just let it go. Although the marriage was stable, distance began to creep between them. Carl covered his growing resentment with smiles and busied himself with his career; Becky was none the wiser. This worked until Susan came into the picture.

Carl did not plan to have an affair. He even resisted the feelings that gradually developed between Susan and him. But he never cut it off, and he never dealt with Becky about his dissatisfaction in their marriage. Predictably, Carl and Susan became intimately involved. After three years of leading a double life, Carl moved out. Becky was shocked. Although she had begun to suspect something was wrong, she was still devastated when her worst fears were proven correct. It was then that Carl told her of his resentments, needs, and desires for her to be different in their relationship. All this came as a complete surprise to Becky.

Carl left Becky, anticipating that Susan would also leave her husband, they would divorce their respective mates, and marry each other. The plan stalled when Susan decided not to leave her husband. For whatever reason, she was not willing to take that step. What was Carl to do? After three months of living alone, he decided to return home to his wife because he couldn't stand the loneliness. Becky was overjoyed at Carl's return and made every effort to be more of what he needed her to be, but things weren't right. The harder she tried, the more frustrated he became. After four months of working on their marriage, Carl was once again seeing Susan. A year later, a second separation occurred.

What happened? What went wrong? Quite simply, Carl's decision to return home was inappropriate. It was the right behavior, but for the wrong reason. He was returning because he was lonely, not because he had any real desire to be with Becky. Second, he had never resolved his motivation for leaving her in the first place. He continued to be emotionally attached to Susan. Until that attachment was resolved, reconciliation could not be achieved and they would not be ready to work on their relationship. No matter what Becky did, improvement would not be made.

My second example involves Jim and Linda. Similar to the previous illustration, this was also a case where a husband was pulled out of the marriage. Unlike Carl, Jim did resolve his motivation to leave Linda when he found that his dream girl wasn't everything he had initially envisioned. With the emotional attachment severed, he headed for home. You might think this had the makings of a genuine reconciliation, and it did. However, its potential was foiled by Jim's attitude and Linda's desperation. Jim wanted to come home, but he wanted to come home on his terms.

"I want to come home, but I don't want to be harassed about the past. I realize that I shouldn't have done what I did, but it's over now. I don't want to hear anything else about it. If you can't forgive and forget and let us start fresh, then forget it. What's it going to be?"

Desperate for the marriage to be restored, Linda took Jim back with open arms. She realized he was not genuinely remorseful and that he was definitely in control of the relationship. She also realized that his behavior had hurt her very badly. But she convinced herself that none of this was really important; all that mattered was the restoration of the marriage. Unfortunately, unless there is reconciliation, there can be no restoration.

Linda thought it wouldn't matter, and it didn't, at first. But after a few weeks of having Jim home, Linda noticed there was a block between them. They couldn't get close. She began to think about what had occurred and how Jim just waltzed back into her arms. Then she began to get angry. This undealt-with and unresolved anger soon turned into resentment. Remember, Jim didn't want to hear anything about the past. "Let's just forget that it ever happened. Let's start fresh." Resentment can be displayed in many different ways. With Linda, it was expressed as emotional coldness. She became aloof and distant. After five more years of marriage, the facade was ended when Jim finally filed for divorce.

So, what am I saying? You shouldn't accept a husband back unless he is totally and absolutely smitten with you? Does he have to grovel on his knees and have definitely rekindled love and adoration? No. This is not what I'm suggesting at all. What I'm suggesting is that there be at least the rudiments of a genuine reconciliation, and that much of this is expressed by his attitude. Specifically, is there any admission of wrongdoing on his part? If so, is there any remorse or genuine sorrow for the pain his behavior caused you? Is he accepting any responsibility for the failure of your marriage? Does he see his contribution, or was it all your fault? Is there a desire and willingness to work on the relationship—past, present, and future—to look at those things that weren't right, deal with the hurts of separation, and rebuild for the future? Or is it, "I'm back. That's it. Let's get on with life"?

As you can see, when it comes to making a decision as to whether a husband can return or not, considering his attitude is of the utmost importance. If he's not coming back for the right reasons, you probably would be ill-advised to let him return. Without genuine reconciliation, there will be no marital restoration.

History of the Relationship

When trying to decide whether a husband should be allowed to return, a primary area of consideration is the history of the relationship. Has the marriage been historically stable? If it had not been for this one incident that prompted the separation, would the marriage be fairly unblemished? Or has this incident been one in a long series of disrupting experiences?

When it comes to evaluating this aspect, we become much more wary when there is a repetitive history of inappropriate behavior. Patterns of misbehavior suggest a greater possibility for deeply ingrained personality problems. At the very least, there's a need for professional evaluation and a possible plan for treatment *before* resuming any type of life together. You will recall that in instances of husbands who are put out, behavioral change needs to be demonstrated over an extended period of time before reconciliation is considered.

Sometimes patterns are blatant and well known prior to the separation. This was the case with Mary and Tim. In their fifteen-year marriage, Tim had been involved with at least twelve other women. He made little effort to hide his behavior from Mary. After he reached an even dozen, Mary put him out. It was at that point that Tim decided he had a problem. Of course, he wanted to come home and work on it.

At other times, patterns of inappropriate behavior are more concealed and it is only during the separation that the wife becomes aware of the deceptive history of her marriage. Such was the case with Kathy and Gerald. Kathy thought her marriage was stable and Gerald was a responsible, faithful husband. It was only after he left that irregularities began to appear: questionable financial dealings, sordid extramarital relationships, new information regarding job changes. Who was this man that Kathy had lived with for all these years? Information came from every direction. She was a classic case of being the last to know.

The point to recognize is this: Whether the pattern of inappropriate marital behavior has been blatant and obvious throughout the duration of the marriage or has been subtle and concealed, the response is the same. Extreme caution is called for. Patterns, as opposed to isolated incidents, call for wariness when considering a husband's return.

Future Expectations for the Relationship

Whereas marital history can point to some fairly obvious flaws, future expectations for the relationship have a far more subtle flair. The usual scenario goes something like this: A husband is either pulled or pushed out of the marriage. For a period of time, he is swinging out of the relationship. But then, for whatever reason, he resolves his motivation for leaving. If it was another woman, he finds that she wasn't what he really wanted. If it was the search for greener pastures, he finds these to be illusive. At any rate, remorseful and wiser, he swings back toward his wife and the marriage. He desires reconciliation.

Everything up to this point is fine. It's exactly what we want to see happen. Where the real rub begins to occur, however, is from here forward. What does the husband want to see happen in his marriage after he returns? Does he have any goals? Does he have any expectations? Frequently, he doesn't. He only wants things to settle down and be as they were because he's ready for some calmness in his life.

You may ask what's wrong with this. What's wrong with things being as they were? The relationship was failing before he left. If it hadn't been, the marital crisis would probably never have occurred. So of what value is it to return to that failing condition, to be "as it was"? If that's what happens, what are the chances of another crisis occurring a little further down the marital road? To avoid this, *things have to be different than they were.*

When I counsel wives during a marital separation, we spend some time defining what constitutes marital health. Emotional honesty, sensitivity, demonstrated caring, vulnerability, willingness to confront, growing intimacy in many of its dimensions—these are just some of the attributes we discuss, all of which are essential for a relationship to be vibrant and growing. As we discuss these characteristics, wives begin to recognize what was not happening in their marriage before the crisis. More importantly, however, they begin to see what has to happen if reconciliation does occur. There is a dawning realization that the marriage can never return to what it once was. It has to be better. They develop expectations.

One of the wives with whom I was working summed up her

feelings about this entire consideration by spontaneously singing a line from an old song: "How're you gonna keep 'em down on the farm, after they've seen Paree?" That one phrase truly captures the essence of this line of reasoning. Having experienced the consequences of what doesn't work and having been exposed to what does, it was difficult for her to give up the expectation of the latter for that of the former.

"I can't go back to the way it was. Tim wants to come home. But he says he'll be happy for us to be the way we were . . . me doing my thing and him doing his. Since I've seen the rules that seemed to control our lives—and just how dysfunctional they were—I realize I can't go back to that."

Now, I'm not saying that you shouldn't take a husband back unless he totally endorses your expectations for the future of the relationship. But I am saying that expectations are a legitimate consideration. They ought to be something the two of you thoroughly discuss. It may be something he has given little thought to. Once enlightened of both the reasons for failure and the essentials for growth, he may share your expectations. However, if what he wants differs greatly from what you want, friction and emotional distance can be expected. It might be best to try and resolve some of the differences before you resume living together.

Willingness to Enter Counseling

Some would see this as an unnecessary adjunct to reconciliation. "We're back together. What need do we have for a counselor?" That's a good question. I think there are two good reasons for seeing a counselor when you are ready to put your marriage back together. The first is to see that you clearly deal with the reconciliatory phase of the relationship; the second is to ensure that you deal with restoration.

Reconciliation can be a painful process. Since we are by nature pain-avoiding creatures, it's easy to miss a few vital points as we come back together. Similar to treating a wound, it is important that the injury be thoroughly cleaned out. We don't need any unresolved issues. The departure created a great deal of pain; there was hurt. This must be thoroughly dealt with and cleansed as forgiveness is sought and extended. We don't need to anxiously skip over the hurt under the guise of not wanting to create any more pain. A counselor will help you stay on the task of genuine reconciliation. Also, it may be that if the motivation for returning is not what it needs to be, this will show up under the scrutiny of the counseling sessions.

Restoration is the other area that can benefit from the skillful hand of a professional counselor. Your relationship was failing before your husband decided to leave, or the crisis would not have occurred. The issues that contributed to that marital condition are still present. Upon the foundation of reconciliation, a relationship can be healed and restored, but this rebuilding process will require you to deal with those things that prevented your marriage from being healthy and growing in the first place. If you tended to avoid conflictual issues earlier in your marriage, it's highly likely you will continue to do so now that you have reconciled. If you inappropriately dealt with anger earlier, you will probably handle it inappropriately now. The old patterns will simply become the new patterns. There is no reason to suspect that anything within your relationship will be different just because you have reconciled. You can easily go on relating just as you did before the crisis, and this could be disastrous.

To give your marriage the best opportunity for restoration, you need to look at what went wrong in your marriage before the crisis occurred. What was your contribution to the failure, and what was that of your husband? You need to correct those tendencies and choose to invest in the relationship, and this is best accomplished with the aid of a good marital therapist.

This is a major point to consider when deciding on whether to allow your husband to return. Is he willing to see a counselor with you, or does he see this as unnecessary? It may not be essential, but I believe it can be a definite aid to reconciling and restoring a marriage.

Making Your Decision

You have a choice to make. Your husband wants to come home. Do you let him or not?

The goal of this chapter has been to aid you in making this decision. After sifting your husband and his request through the four considerations I have outlined here, how does he fare? Do things look fairly positive? His attitude is good, the marital history was not repetitively blemished, he wants more than the relationship offered before the separation, and there is a willingness for counseling. Or does he fall short in one or more of these areas? Is he, in fact, not yet ready to come home? Remember, you have a say in this decision, and your decision needs to be based on the ultimate best interest of your marriage.

If your answer is yes, the most difficult task before you will be to forgive and trust him again. You must be willing to take him at face value. Not doing this will only frustrate the healing process.

I've worked with couples where forgiveness, or the lack of it, periodically resurfaced as a problem in the marriage. With one particular couple, every time the old incident was brought into the present, the marriage was again placed in jeopardy.

"I don't know what it is. But I can't get it out of my mind. There isn't anything that he's done. But I think of his involvement with her, and all the pain that it caused me, and I get mad. I can't help it."

"I don't know what else to do. I've told her I was wrong—I shouldn't have done it. But sorrys don't seem to help. What can I do? How long is this going to go on? We're not getting anywhere like this. Maybe we should just call it quits."

For other couples, forgiveness isn't the problem because angry incidents don't resurface. However, there is a great deal of difficulty when it comes to trusting the returned husband. Odometers are checked, repeated questions regarding schedules and whereabouts are asked, and some men are even followed or physically checked up on.

Whether it is unforgiveness or distrust, the result is blockage in the restoration of the marriage. If you decide to take him back, you must do so all the way. Deal with the separation, then let it go. Deal with the issue of trust. Recognize that he cannot do enough to earn your complete trust. He can destroy it, but he can't earn it. It is something you will have to *give*. Also recognize that if he's going to be untrustworthy, it's only a matter of time before you find out. Somehow these things do not remain secret. So give your marriage a chance. Decide to forgive and trust.

If your answer is no, the most difficult task before you will be holding to your belief that you are doing the right thing for the right reason. *No* is typically based on the assessment that your husband is not yet truly ready to return. He may want to come home, but he's not yet ready to do so healthily, in a way that would lead toward genuine reconciliation. His attitude is wrong, or the marital history suggests a wary watchfulness is warranted, etc.

You must firmly believe in the appropriateness of your decision, because saying no will bring a great deal of pressure from your husband. Remember, in his mind, he is ready to come home and you are the one interfering with the resumption of the marriage. This pressure may come indirectly, by way of family members and friends who will tell you that the right thing to do in a case like this is to take him back. Or it may come more directly from your husband. Here is an example of a highly manipulative approach: "I'm ready to return. If this marriage ends now, it's because of you. It will be all your fault. You will be to blame."

Holding out for a true reconciliation will not be easy. There will be many pressures for you to settle for less. But remember, ultimately it is your choice, and you will have to live with the consequences.

Study Questions

1. What are both your and your spouse's motivations for ending the separation? Are these "healthy motivations"?

2. What are your future expectations of the relationship?

3. Are both of you willing to enter counseling? If not, why not?

4. Do you think it's time for your spouse to come home? Be honest.

Your Response

_____

_____

_____

_____

_____

_____

_____

12

Husbands Who Don't Come Home

Carol and Steve had been separated for eight months. I became involved with the situation shortly after Steve left. Carol had been taken by total surprise when her husband of twelve years suddenly decided to leave the marriage and set up housekeeping on his own. In a dazed and confused condition, Carol sought my advice on what she should do.

With work, Carol was able to successfully let Steve go. It was difficult because she thought she needed him so much, but with determination and a plan of action in hand, she proceeded to do what she thought was in the best interest of the relationship. Carol stated her declaration, removed the comfort zone, backed off, and resisted the temptation to pursue him. She had done all the right things, but here we were, eight months down the road and nothing had changed. Steve was still swinging out of the marriage, and there was nothing to suggest that there was any change in sight. Why? Why hadn't Steve returned to the marriage?

"I've been letting Steve go for eight months now. But nothing's happened. Nothing has changed. What's going on? I'm really growing tired of well-doing. Why hasn't he come back?"

There is a point that needs to be clarified about the let-him-go philosophy. Even though the primary goal of letting a husband go is to bring genuine reconciliation to the relationship, of even greater significance is that we are *doing the right thing.* In a very real sense, we let a husband go for ourselves. We cannot control what he will do. He may choose to continue irresponsibly. But even if he does, we can at least control our own behavior.

We do the right thing because we are responsible people. In the case of letting a husband go, it is hoped that this will help bring reconciliation to the relationship. In fact, it is my personal belief that this approach offers the best opportunity for a genuine reconciliation. But there are no guarantees this will happen. Sometimes husbands come home; other times, they don't. But regardless, we do what is right.

Why Husbands Don't Come Home

Even when you let them go, sometimes husbands don't come home. When this occurs, it is generally because of one of three reasons. Clarifying why husbands don't come home will help us to know what to do.

They Have Not Yet Resolved Their Motivation for Leaving

Whether he was pulled out, pushed out, or put out, the motivation that prompted his departure has not been resolved. In the case of a pulled-out husband, he is still pursuing the other woman. With the pushed-out husband, he is still pursuing greener pastures and continues to see home as a frustrating place to be. And with the put-out husband, he is still pursuing selfish, irresponsible behavior over the legitimate needs of others. Until he resolves his motivation for leaving, a husband will not be ready to swing back into the marriage.

This failure to resolve the motivation for leaving is what kept Steve swinging out of the marriage even though Carol was doing all the right things. He had been pulled out by an affair. Although he initially protested that this was not the case, it quickly became evident that there was another woman involved. Because she was married, they found it legally expedient to deny the relationship. Once it was discovered and it could no longer be denied, Steve admitted to the affair. However, he then claimed that the extramarital involvement was over. The other woman had supposedly decided to reconcile with her husband. But Steve was not ready to come home. This is where things had stood for the last six months of their eight-month separation.

Why wasn't Steve ready to come home? Even though he claimed the affair had ended, it hadn't; he and his girlfriend had only become far more careful. With his motivation to leave still unresolved, Carol's doing the right thing had not produced the desired results.

Before Steve could be ready to return home, he would have to end the affair. The same can be said for pushed-out husbands. The search for greener pastures and the desire to avoid dealing with what has been a frustrating marriage has to be resolved before there is the possibility for reconciliation. Pushing this reason for why husbands fail to return a little further, it is also applicable to husbands who are put out. A put-out husband must resolve his irresponsibility before he is truly ready to return. If he doesn't, he can no more swing back toward the marriage than his pulled-out and pushed-out counterparts. The motivation for leaving must be resolved. Failure to achieve this is what keeps some husbands from returning to their marriages.

They View the Marriage as Emotionally Dead

This particular reason for failing to return is mostly applicable to pulled-out and pushed-out husbands. The affair has ended, or the fantasized greener pastures have been found to be full of thorns, but these husbands conclude there just isn't anything worth returning to. At least there's nothing worth the effort. One pulled-out husband put it this way:

> I'm no longer involved with Linda. That ended about as quickly as it got started. We had gone from being acquaintances to being an item in about a week. We lived together on an emotional high for three months after I finally left Joan. Then zap—the whole relationship went flat. After a couple of weeks of trying to regain speed, we both decided to forget it. If it wasn't going to come naturally, then there didn't seem to be much point in trying to keep it together. So we went separate directions.
>
> I asked myself the question, "What do I do now?" That was when I thought about going home to Joan. I knew she wanted me back, but I just couldn't do it. Emotionally, whatever I had for Joan was dead. I guess we were just too incompatible. Whatever the reason, since I had already made the break, I figured I might as well keep on going. I just wasn't willing to go back and work on something that seemed so dead.

Even though the pull was resolved, this husband could not bring himself to return home. His resolution had to occur before he *could* return home, but it did not mean that he necessarily *would* go back to his former relationship. A pushed-out husband put it this way:

> Jean and I fought for fifteen years before I moved out. I thought she was trying to control me, and she thought I was trying to control her. Who knows? Maybe we both were in the wrong. At any rate, I felt so frustrated and trapped that I couldn't stand it any longer.

The single life sure seemed appealing to me then. Being alone would bring some peace into my life, and I was certain that there was an ample and easily accessible supply of women who wouldn't want to control me. At least, this was what I envisioned. It didn't take long for reality to set in. Being alone turned to loneliness. As for all the available women, they must have gone into hiding when I separated from Jean, because they were nowhere to be found.

When the mirage of the greener pastures disappeared before my very eyes, I began to think about going home. That would solve some of my problems. But as I began to reminisce about the years we spent together and all the pain we inflicted on each other, I realized that I couldn't do it. Unless it was going to be easy— unless there was some guarantee that things would be different—I couldn't go back. As disappointed as I was with the single life-style, I could not return to an unsatisfactory marriage. And since no one was willing to offer me any guarantees, Jean and I divorced.

This husband resolved his motivation for leaving; at least he realized that his vision of greener pastures was more illusion than fact. Yet this wasn't enough to bring him back. Jean had let him go, and he had resolved the push enough to see the outside world realistically and to look back toward home. But he chose not to return. Sometimes, this happens. It is unfortunate, but sometimes husbands simply refuse to come home.

They Are Unwilling to Get Help and Change

This reason for failing to return home is primarily applicable to put-out husbands. Although there is some overlap between this reason and the first one I described, where the motivation behind the separation has been irresponsible behavior and this has failed to be resolved, its significant importance warrants special consideration.

Sometimes the unwillingness to deal with personal irresponsibility is blatant and challenging. This is illustrated by these comments from an alcoholic husband: "You knew I drank when you married me. There's nothing wrong with it. If we stay married, you're going to have to accept me the way I am."

The fact that he was intoxicated more than he was sober, that he could not keep a job, and that his behavior was creating an undue amount of stress on all the family members seemed to make little difference to him. All that mattered was his desire to drink, and he was definitely unwilling to get help for something he didn't see as a problem.

Ironically, this blatant and challenging form of unwillingness to get help is actually easier to deal with than its more devious variant form: the husband who admits to having a problem and to his willingness to seek help for it but fails to follow through on his reported good intentions.

I counseled a couple whose particular form of irresponsible behavior was physical abuse. After repeated offenses, numerous trips to the emergency room, and finally the fear of the abuse spreading to the children, Mary put Chuck out of the house. He immediately sought to return home, claiming to have changed. Following a let-him-go plan of action, Mary resolutely stood her ground. She stated a list of expectations that needed to be met before any serious discussion of reconciliation could be entered.

The list Mary presented to Chuck was more than reasonable and included successful involvement in a therapy program for physical abusers. Chuck was irate. He refused to seek counseling, claiming to have mastered his problem, and said he would sooner be divorced than submit to this waste of time and money. Mary informed him that she was not responsible for the choices he made. Whether he was to seek counseling or not was obviously one of those things he would have to decide. However, she was responsible for the choices she made, and she had recently made the decision that she would no longer live in an abusive relationship. That was her choice. Based on the history of her marriage, as well as her newly acquired knowledge regarding physically abusive men, Mary knew she could not have a physically safe marriage unless Chuck had professional help. If Chuck refused to get help, then he was choosing a divorce.

As the events of this story continued, Chuck tried by every conceivable means to change Mary's direction. He begged, sabotaged, and harassed. Nothing swayed Mary from her chosen course of action. At last, less than a week before the divorce was to be final, Chuck agreed to see a counselor if Mary would call a halt to the divorce. Attorneys conferred, and the divorce proceedings were interrupted. Chuck was given four months to locate a counselor, become involved in an appropriate treatment program, and demonstrate at least a change in direction, if not significant improvement.

During the four-month stay of proceedings, Chuck constantly tried to get back into the marriage, but he made no attempt to get professional help for his abusive tendencies. As the four months lapsed and divorce proceedings were again instituted, Chuck finally called a therapist. Although frustrated, Mary once again agreed to an interruption in divorce proceedings in order to allow Chuck an opportunity to get help. Unfortunately, his pattern repeated. After three more months of waiting, Chuck had yet to see a therapist for a single session, much less become actively involved in an appropriate treatment program. Amidst pleas for another chance, Mary finally divorced Chuck.

Although Chuck's refusal to get help for his personal problems was not as blatant and challenging as my first example, it was just as deliberate. As sad as it may be, husbands who refuse to change their irresponsible behavior are in a very real sense choosing not to return to their marriages. When this occurs, wives who are seeking genuine reconciliation are left with very few options.

What to Do

What do you do about husbands who don't come home? Do you treat them all the same, or are there factors that suggest one course of action in some situations and another in others?

Although the frequent answer to the question, "What do you do when your husband fails to return home?" is *Get on with your life,* there are qualifying factors that sometimes negate this response. For instance, what if your husband leaves you for another woman and you decide to work toward reconciliation by following the let-him-go philosophy, but after only three weeks of letting him go, you decide to get on with your life because he has failed to return to the marriage? He hasn't resolved his motivation for leaving, but has there been an adequate length of time to make such a major decision? Probably not. This would be one of those situations where the extenuating circumstance of time would need to be considered. Sure, the reason for his failure to return is clearly known. But rather than getting on with your life, a more appropriate response would be to continue the let-him-go philosophy for a while longer.

There are some other extenuating circumstances, but they are few in number. The important point here is this: When you come to the place where you realize your husband is not coming home, the only healthy course of action remaining for you is to *get on with your life.*

This is never an easy decision to make, but when husbands

don't come home, there's little else for you to do. You could continue to hang on to the relationship, but this only prolongs your pain. There comes a time when you have to let the marriage go if you are going to heal. This, too, will be painful, but I believe the Lord is redemptive in our circumstances. God always has a future for His people, and "in all things" His hope, peace, and direction can be found.

Two issues that aid you in getting on with your life are acceptance and forgiveness. *Acceptance* is one of those terms I hear a lot, but what does it mean in relation to husbands who don't come home? Basically, you are accepting as fact what has become painfully evident: The relationship has ended. It is over. This isn't saying that things couldn't have ended differently or that this is how things *should* be. It definitely isn't how you *wanted* them to be. But it is an acceptance of reality, and this sense of finality marks a necessary turning point in your healing. With acceptance, you begin to get on with your life. You begin to move from the nebulous confusion and chaos that has dominated your life to order and sanity. It will take a while, but you've started the journey.

Another necessary part of letting go of the relationship and getting on with your life is forgiveness of yourself and your husband. All the things that you should have done but didn't—you've got to let them go. All the things that you did but shouldn't have—you've got to let them go. All of your own personal contributions to the marital deterioration—you've got to let them go. Sure, if you had it to do all over again, you'd probably do all those things you should have done and wouldn't do those things you shouldn't have done, and. . . . But what's the use? You don't have it to do all over again, so let it go. Stop beating yourself to death. This isn't a form of denial. No one is denying that you messed up, but now it's time to get on with things.

Forgiveness also needs to be extended to your husband. This is not an acceptance of his behavior. Whether he wants it or not, you need to be free of him, and that only comes with forgiveness. In spite of what he has done, as long as you hold bitterness and resentment for him, you remain tied to him. You are only released when you forgive. This is difficult to do and frequently needs to be a cognitive decision because you do not feel forgiving. Make it a matter of prayer. The feeling of forgiveness and emotional release from the relationship may come some time after the cognitive decision has been made, but it will start with the intent to do the right thing.

So what do you do when your husband doesn't come home? You get on with your life. Is it easy? No. Is it necessary? Yes. Can you do it? Absolutely!

Study Questions

1. Why do you think your husband does not want to come home?

2. What should be your next step?

3. What needs to happen for you to accept that your spouse is not coming home?

4. In what ways do you need to forgive your spouse for his actions? Or vice-versa?

5. What are your plans for getting on with your life? Begin formulating them here.

Your Response

13

How Long Do You Wait?

Sometimes husbands come home, sometimes they don't. When they don't, how long do you wait before getting on with your life?

This is a difficult question to answer. Part of our difficulty rests with the pull of both theoretical and practical living. Theoretically, there is always a chance that your husband will come back to the marriage. Whether he finally comes to his senses or God finally breaks in upon him, there is always a theoretical chance for reconciliation. But we do not live in a theoretical world. We live in a world of flesh and blood. When the problems of everyday life cut across our very being, our pain is real, not theoretical. And it is to this reality that we ultimately must respond.

Practically speaking, when waiting for husbands to return home, we ultimately reach a point where believing that there is "always a chance" becomes "hanging on," where letting him go and doing the right thing only prolong the inevitable, where it's better for all concerned that you cut the marriage loose and get on with your life. But when is this point reached?

If you are looking for a specific length of time to use as a measuring stick, I'm afraid you're going to be disappointed. There is no such rule of thumb. I cannot tell you how long to wait. At least, I cannot give you a length of time that would be applicable to every situation. For some of you, a year would be too long; for others, a year would not be long enough. Different circumstances require different actions, so I can't tell you when you've waited long enough. But I can suggest some factors to consider that can serve as indicators for your decision making.

Are You Emotionally Ready?

Within reason, I believe that people need to do what they are *ready* to do. There are some exceptions to this belief. Sometimes our weaknesses interfere with our getting ready. At other times, changing external circumstances require that we do something we may not be totally prepared to do. But by and large, we need to do what we are ready to do.

When it comes to marital relationships, I find there is a natural progression toward emotional disengagement during a separation. This is fairly understandable. The marital crisis brings a great deal of emotional pain. There may be shock and numbness at the outset, but this quickly gives way to hurt, loneliness, and anger. We cannot persist in this emotional turmoil. It must be resolved, and it generally is. Either you reconcile with your husband, thus bringing healing to your relationship and elimination of the precipitant of the pain, or you begin to protectively disengage. By *disengage* I mean that you emotionally distance and withdraw from your husband, thereby eliminating the pain. You begin to accept the separation and dissolve some of the emotional ties that have been binding the two of you together. You do this naturally. There is no real premeditation involved, only a need to survive.

During this natural process of disengagement, a number of changes takes place. On an emotional level, you gradually move from feeling despondent to being very angry to disengaging. Although these changes are not clearly marked separations, the percentage of mixture between despondency

214

and anger changes. You become less despondent and more angry. Eventually, both of these diminish as disengagement proceeds. The behavioral component that accompanies this emotional progression is a change from being strongly reactive to behaving according to rational decision-making processes.

The actions of one of my clients will serve as an illustration of this entire disengagement process. I had been counseling Mary for two months, although she had been separated for five. John had left her for another woman. As is typical in these situations, Mary unsuccessfully pursued John when he left. In utter confusion, she came to my office. I began coaching her to let him go, and for two months she had been trying to do all the right things. Then she came in and made the following declaration:

"I'm tired of this. John makes me so mad. I want a divorce. If he doesn't want me, then I don't want him. I can do better."

To say the least, Mary was extremely angry. She didn't really want a divorce. What she really wanted was for John to come home, but he hadn't, and she was mad. Ironically, the two months of prior sessions had found Mary much more despondent, but things were beginning to change. I would rather have a client mad than sad. It seems to be easier for them to do what needs to be done when they're mad. But the progression from one phase to another is always an indication that disengagement is under way. Eventually, Mary did divorce John. He never resolved his motivation for leaving (the other woman). But when she did divorce him, it was an action, not a reaction. She moved from despondency to anger to disengagement (from reacting to acting) and then out. Mary was ready to get on with her life.

So why is it so difficult to determine whether or not you're ready to get on with your life? If you're ready, then where's the problem? The problem is that you never get totally ready. At least you never get to the point where getting on with your life is an easy decision. It may be the best decision, but it will not be easy. Getting ready is more a matter of degree than it is a clear and distinct destination. Through the natural disengagement process, you gradually become readier, and eventually you become ready enough. But you never become completely ready. It is never that easy.

How Long Have You Waited?

Even though I cannot give you an exact length of time, there are probably some extremes on both ends of the continuum that need to be avoided. A key term that would capsulize this entire concept is the word *ample.* There needs to be ample time to honestly let your husband go. A few weeks would not be a sufficient length of time; a few years would be excessive. As we move from these two extremes, we approach what could be considered an ample length of time.

A second point to be considered in this issue of time is the quality of the time that has taken place since your husband left. If he left one year ago but you have been pursuing him throughout the entirety of the separation, this time has been fairly nonproductive. We would view this situation far differently had you been letting him go for the past year. You have to get time working for you, and this doesn't happen until you begin to do healthy, constructive things about the separation. When you take your stand, make your declaration, and begin to let him go, time begins to work for you, but not until. So when you start to ask yourself the question, "Have I waited an ample length of time?" you also have to ask the questions, "How much of this separation has been constructive? How long has time been working for me?" It's only in addressing both of these areas that the question of time can be answered.

Have You Done All You Know to Do?

One of the standard questions I ask whenever I counsel with a couple for the first time is, "What have you done in an attempt to deal with your problem?" Frequently, their answer is "Nothing." At least they have done nothing constructive. Yet all too often these same couples, who have done little or nothing to deal constructively with their marital dissatisfaction, are unwilling to exert much effort to change things. I don't find this very responsible behavior. Giving up before you have exerted constructive effort—before you have done all you know to do—is irresponsible, and being irresponsible is not the goal toward which we strive.

A similar position can be taken with the issue of marital separation. Your husband has left. That's a fact. Have you waited long enough for him to come back? I don't know. As we are discovering, there seem to be a number of questions that need to be answered before that decision can be made. One of these questions has to do with your behavior during this time of separation. Have you been responsible, or have you been irresponsible? Have you done all you know to do, or are there things that are left undone?

I worked with one wife who had been through an extremely painful separation. Her husband had left her for another woman, then returned home for a few months, only to leave once again for the same woman. When he left the first time, this wife pursued him in the hope of winning him back. She thought that was the Christian thing to do. When he left the second time, she came to me for advice regarding divorce. I began to explore the history of her marriage and the events of her separation. Divorce was obviously an option. However, as we discussed what she had done during the separation thus far, it became quite clear that there were some constructive

217

activities she had failed to do. For instance, she had never followed a let-him-go plan of action. She had only pursued him and allowed him to come home without genuinely dealing with his motivation for returning. I challenged her to let him go—to do all she knew to do—before she made the decision to get on with her life. She agreed.

Responsibility is one of the reasons we do all we know to do, but there is another. When all is said and done, if your husband does not return home, you need to be able to walk away from the marriage with no regrets. Actually, you can probably never walk away without regrets, but you can walk away with fewer regrets if you do all that you know to do. In the case that I just described, the wife began to constructively let her husband go. We worked together to deal with all the things that would interfere with her doing what she needed to do. But even though she did all the right things, he did not return. Finally, she was ready to get on with her life. She went to him and explained that she could no longer live as they had lived. If he wanted to deal with their relationship, she would postpone any legal action, but this was his last chance. He refused, and she divorced him.

When this wife first came to me, she was not truly ready to get on with her life. She was tired of things the way they were, but she wasn't ready to move on. After doing everything she knew to do, and realizing it, she became ready to move on. She had some regrets, but these were in the area of "what could have been." She had no regrets regarding her attempts to reconcile the marriage. She had done all that she knew to do. She had no other choice left but to get on with her life.

What about you? Have you done all that you know to do, or are you avoiding your responsible behavior? Not only does behaving responsibly offer you the best opportunity for positive results, but it also prepares you to move on with your life if this is what has to happen.

Have You Realistically Assessed Your Situation?

Let's face reality. What's your real situation? Sure, he may come back, but have you been telling yourself that for two months or two years? Have you been totally irresponsible in your behavior, or have you done all the right things? Exactly what is your situation? Getting perspective on your situation requires that you assess it realistically.

What is reality, anyway? Anything is possible, but does that make it reality? Not at all. When it comes to realistically assessing your situation, you have to begin to deal with probabilities, not possibilities. In essence, you have to define your own reality. Based on a number of factors, what is real for you?

In realistically assessing your situation, you need to consider the following factors:

History of the Relationship

Is the current crisis in your marriage an incident, or is it more reflective of a pattern? Has the quality of your marriage been good, or has there always been conflict and dissension? Is your husband's current behavior reflective of some long-standing personality deficiencies, or is he a fairly emotionally stable individual? What has been the history of your relationship? History can be a fair predictor of the future.

Time of Separation

How much time has transpired since your husband left? Has it been a few weeks, a few months, or a few years? The longer things persist, the less hopeful they appear.

Current Status

What's currently happening? Is he just as involved with the other woman? Just as frustrated with the thought of returning home? Just as irresponsible in his behavior? Or have there been some significant changes to warrant a glimmer of hope? How do things stand now, and how does that compare to the amount of time you have been separated?

Your Behavior

Have you behaved responsibly and constructively? Have you done all you know to do? Or have you been pursuing him the entire time?

Looking at these factors, how does your reality begin to shape up? What is the probability that things will ever change? Is there enough doubt in these areas to warrant waiting a while longer, or are things fairly clear? Once you determine your reality, you need to act accordingly.

Are You Being Forced to Act?

Sometimes you are forced to act before you are ready. You haven't disengaged emotionally, there hasn't been an ample period of time, you haven't done everything that you know to do, and reality is elusive. Still, you must act. Why?

Although there is probably more than one reason for acting before you're ready, the primary instance where this would occur regards the issue of protection. This may be either self-protection or the protection of your children, and it involves both physical and financial security. Let me share with you some case studies to illustrate my point. In one case, the wife was more than willing to give her pulled-out husband some time to resolve his motivation for leaving, but he refused to provide any financial support for the family. After three months of this, facing the real probability of losing their home if things did not change, she had no recourse but to begin legal action to force him to be financially responsible. This was a protective move. In another instance, a wife was forced to act because she saw their entire life savings dwindling away. He was spending it all. Faced with the real probability of financial ruin, she had to act. Again, this was a protective move. It was not something that she wanted to do. In fact, she was trying very diligently to let her husband go, but his irresponsibility would not allow her to pursue this course of action. She was forced to act.

We see the same line of reasoning applicable to physical safety. I have worked with countless wives who have put their husbands out because of physical abuse or alcoholism, only to find they could not keep them out. If their husbands had willingly stayed away, ceased harassment, and gotten professional help, these wives could have allowed time to pass, but the husbands continued in their irresponsible patterns. They forced the issue, which left their wives with little recourse but to proceed with legal action. This kind of problem is frequently seen in regard to children. One controlling and demanding husband reacted to being put out by taking the children while his wife was at work. He returned them after a few days of "vacation" but indicated that he would do it again until she "came to her senses" and returned home. They were his children, too, and he had just as much right to them as she did. "There's not a thing you can do about it." He was right. Short of legal intervention and custody determination, there wasn't anything she could do, so she filed for divorce. She wasn't ready to file, but she was forced to.

Getting on with your life is a difficult enough decision to make when you are ready to do it. Making the decision because you are forced to is even more difficult. Maybe the actual decision isn't any more difficult. After all, what choice do you have? But the adjustment seems to be more difficult. In the final analysis, we do what we need to do.

Indications That You Have Waited Long Enough

As I said at the outset of this chapter, I cannot tell you exactly when you have waited long enough. When it is right for you to get on with your life will be different for each of you and based on differing circumstances. However, there are indications that suggest you may be ready to make this decision:

- Do you feel ready to get on with your life?
- Have you given the situation an ample and constructive period of time?
- Have you done everything that you know to do in order to reconcile your marriage?
- Based on a realistic assessment of your situation, is the probability of your husband's return very low?
- For the protection of yourself and/or your children, are you being forced to act?

Answering these questions should give you an indication as to whether you have waited long enough or not. If your answers were mostly affirmative, then maybe it's time to get on with your life. If your answers were primarily no, then you're probably not ready. If this is the case, at least you have some direction to pursue. You know the questions that have to be answered yes before you will be ready, so work on those areas.

Regardless of your decision, let me reaffirm that making the break will not be easy. It may be right, but it will not be easy. As you move toward getting on with your life, elicit the help of concerned others. You will find a support network to be of immense aid.

Study Questions

1. Have you done all you know to do to work towards reconciliation?

2. What is your current assessment of the situation?

3. How does the history of your relationship relate to any hope for the future?

4. How long have you been separated?

5. What, in your opinion, is the current status of the relationship?

6. Have you waited long enough? Describe your feelings in detail.

Your Response

_____

_____

_____

_____

_____

_____

_____

_____

_____

_____